FOREWORD

Scottish skiing is different. Alpine exponents with years of experience will find that the sport that they thought they knew all about is not Scottish skiing. Our maritime climate; our geological background; our development that originated from skiers themselves, has resulted in a brand of the sport that is unique!

That is why this book is necessary. In Scotland, skiing is a way of life rather than a sport. Anyone who skis here is taking on the mountains. The Arctic explorer would often be more at home on our slopes than the most able resort exponent from abroad. Armed with this book, however, new enthusiasts can join the band of people who come alive in the winter. They need the right information so that they wear the correct clothes for our weather, the appropriate equipment for our icy and windswept slopes and, of course, they need to know 'where to go'.

Then, they will find that Scottish skiing can give fantastic rewards! The best days of my life have been on Scottish hills. Anyone who loves to feel the wind in their hair and an adventure round the corner will find that Scottish skiing can give them this too. But they need to know the ropes.....with this book in their rucksack, they will be OK!

MYRTLE SIMPSON

.....shudder and scuttle hastily back to bed.

SCOTTISH SKIING HANDBOOK

HILARY PARKE

First Edition 1989.

SCOTTISH

SKIING

HANDBOOK

By

Hilary Parke

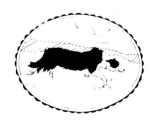

Luath Press LTD.

Acknowledgments

This handbook would never have reached maturity had it not been for the much-appreciated support of the many people who willingly made available such a vast fund of information.

There is, unfortunately, not room to list them all, but I should especially like to mention the following:

The directors, managers and staff of all the Scottish ski centres, downhill and Nordic alike, for their time and co-operation in gathering vital information; Mr G.J. Stewart, former Senior Orthopaedic Registrar at Dundee Royal Infirmary, now at Warrington General Hospital, and Mr A.R. Innes, Senior Orthopaedic Registrar at Dundee Royal Infirmary, for access to the excellent Stewart/Waldie report 'Ski Injuries in Scotland'; Alan C.Souter, Graham Nicoll and Bob Gatling, all experienced 'old hands' who contributed the detailed area descriptions of Cairngorm, The Lecht and Glencoe; Mr John Arnold of the Scottish National Ski Council, for his contribution to the racing section; Dr Helen Ross, Reader in Psychology at Stirling University, who compiled the list of Gaelic place names; Myrtle Simpson, who ploughed bravely through the draft manuscript and made many valuable comments and suggestions; to the individuals, clubs, ski schools, ski-related businesses, tourist organisations and conservation bodies who gave practical help and encouragement, and to Stephen Grieve of Crail Pottery, who was the catalyst for the original idea.

Thanks also to the Scottish Sports Council and the Countryside Commission for permission to reproduce their Scottish Mountain Code.

I also owe a special debt of gratitude to my long-suffering family, who have never once complained about the non-appearance of meals and the lack of clean socks, and without whose self-reliance and support the book would definitely not have become a reality.

CONTENTS

PART ONE

FOREWORD by Myrtle Simpson

PART TWO

THE SCOTTISH DOWNHILL
SKI CENTRES

Mileage Chart. Tourist Information Centres. Bibliography/Reading
List. Useful Addresses. Tables of injuries on Scottish ski slopes.

INTRODUCTION

Scottish skiing has a character all of its own.   This can also be said of those who indulge in it.

There are countless days every winter when normal sane folk, after a brief glance through the window, shudder and scuttle hastily back to bed.

Skiers, however, lack this innate sense of self-preservation. Feverishly they scramble into the sort of garish garb their grandmothers would faint over, bolt down their bowls of muesli, throw their skis in the car and head doggedly for the hills.

Each of these hardy perennials is willing, if not downright keen, to risk life and limb on icy roads, plough through intimidating snowdrifts, and ignore cosy hostelries selling real ale, in order to queue for the privilege of setting his or her own two planks on their chosen piste, or to slog up mile after mile of wind-blasted hillside to 'get away from it all'.

The weather, it must be admitted, is not always perfect.   Why am I doing this? is a question that crops up surprisingly often, usually when under the penetrating assault of millions of needles of ice driven by a 70mph gale, or dragging one's shattered body out of yet another wet snowdrift.   Why indeed?

Plough through intimidating snowdrifts......

1

Crazy and unique Scottish skiing

The answer, if there is one, is different for each individual. Maybe it's those few precious moments when suddenly, magically, it all comes together and your skis finally do just what you want them to, or perhaps it's the unexpected glimpse of a vast white amphitheatre of peaks you never knew existed. For some it's the glorious discovery one morning of a whole corrie of gleaming fresh snow where no-one else has skied, a truly heady dose of the powerful and totally addictive drug to which thousands of us fall prey every year.

Those of us who are mad enough to have skied the Scottish hills under all conditions, in every conceivable kind of weather, have often discussed the things we know now which we wish we had known at the beginning, or even part way along. It wouldn't have deterred us, and we would probably have made some of the same mistakes and lived to tell the tale, but we would almost certainly have spent less time floundering, falling and getting frustrated with lift queues, and a lot more thinking 'Wow — so this is what it's all about!'

Every skiing trip, Nordic or downhill, whether for a day or a fortnight, takes organisation, effort and money. The aim of this handbook, therefore, is to help everyone maximise the time they have available, so that days spent on the hills are thoroughly memorable for all the right reasons, and hopefully also perhaps to convert still more of the unsuspecting British public to the varied, crazy and unique but never boring pursuit of Scottish skiing.

Those of us who are mad enough.......

CHAPTER ONE
TO SKI OR NOT TO SKI - THE REPORTS

For those of us who can think of better ways of spending a Saturday morning than staring at a set of closed snow gates, the reports can save a lot of time, petrol and frustration.

This is not to suggest that ski reports should be regarded as infallible: the most they can do is tell you what conditions were like at the time they were issued, so for this reason it's wise to go for the most up-to-date service available (see details below). After that it's a case of turning to the weather forecasts, or your crystal ball, whichever you trust the most.

It's perfectly normal for the road to be blocked first thing and cleared as a matter of routine. Only when there's been an exceptionally big 'drop' or the blizzard continues to rage on through the morning do real problems arise. Very high winds and/or heavy snowfall fill the roads in as fast as they can be cleared and the crews are forced to wait for a break in the weather before there is any point in continuing. The frustrated skier's only consolation on such days is that the skiing conditions would have been utterly filthy even if he had got there. Chairlifts are unable to run in high winds, and the more exposed tows may also be off in bad weather.

Many radio stations, both national and regional, relay ski and weather reports from quite ungodly hours in the morning, so decisions about the day can be made without even getting out of bed, plus the added appeal of considerable savings on the telephone bill. Ceefax (Page 193) contains a section covering all the Scottish downhill centres and includes a weather forecast, skiing conditions, the state of the runs, which tows are open and whether the access roads are passable.

Crews are forced to wait for a break in the weather

USEFUL TELEPHONE NUMBERS

The snow reports and weather information numbers can be exceedingly useful, provided a few basic pointers are heeded. Always take note of the time of issue of a report: if it was issued the previous evening conditions may well have changed drastically. Try to get the most recent update possible, but be warned, the '0898...' information numbers are charged at fairly hefty rates, particularly at peak periods, so radio and teletext reports may work out cheaper if you do a lot of skiing.

The term 'freezing level' (FL) does not refer to the bits of one's anatomy which feel the cold first. It does, in fact, give clues for assessing snow and weather conditions. The lower the FL the longer the runs will keep their snow/ice and the colder the air temperature will be. The FL tends to rise during the day, often to well above the summits, and this will be accompanied by a corresponding softening of the piste.

'Vertical runs' (thankfully not a form of skier's dysentery) are measured in feet at present, though no doubt one day they will go metric and confuse us all. The figure indicates the length of uninterrupted piste down which it is possible to ski, and once you know your run lengths, gives a good indication of how well the snow is holding. At the end of the season in particular, a substantial overnight drop in the VR length probably means one of the main low-level runs has expired from lack of snow.

SKI HOTLINE - General Outlook - 0898 654 654

Can usually be relied on to tell the truth. They provide quite chatty information on road and snow conditions. The first report is issued as early as possible, usually between 5.30 and 7am, along with an assessment of the weather prospects. There are updates through the day and any major changes, e.g. roads being opened or closed, are put out immediately.

7

SKI HOTLINE - Specific Area Reports

Cairngorm	0898 654 655
Glenshee	0898 654 656
The Lecht	0898 654 657
Glencoe	0898 654 658
Cross Country	0898 654 659
Aonach Mor	0898 654 660
Dalwhinnie Corries	0898 654 661

SKICALL - 0898 500 440
All the Scottish downhill ski areas are covered, a synopsis of snow conditions being given for each one, plus a weather forecast and general outlook from the Glasgow Weather Centre.
CAIRNGORM - 0479 811000/ 041 248 5757
This is the report specific to the Cairngorm ski area and is put out early in the morning, with updates as necessary.
GLENSHEE CHAIRLIFT - 03383 628 (033 9741 628 after Telecom Change)
The Chairlift Company's own recorded announcement on snow and weather conditions: this includes such information as the temperature in the car park, conditions on the access roads and an indication of which lifts they expect to run. It is updated if conditions change radically.
LECHT SKI REPORT - 09754 240 (09756 51440 after Telecom Change)
This is the Ski Centre's own 24 hr. recorded announcement service, with three lines, kept as up to date as possible, and changed if the situation alters drastically.
GLENCOE CHAIRLIFT - 08552 303.
A 24hr recorded announcement on the prevailing snow conditions. Updates are given to Ski Hotline and the Glasgow Weather Centre as and when relevant.

8

CROSS-COUNTRY SKIING CONDITIONS
SKI HOTLINE - 0898 654 659
ACHNASHEEN AREA - 044 588 202
BEN NEVIS & GLENCOE AREA - 0397 4921
CAIRNGORM - 0479 810729 (24hrs)
CLASHINDARROCH - 0466 4161/2734
COCKBRIDGE & UPPER DON AREA - 097 54 240
GLENISLA - 057 582 238/207
GLENMULLIACH - 080 74 356
LOWER STRATHSPEY/DUFFTOWN AREA - 0340 20892
TOMINTOUL & LECHT AREA - 080 74 356

WEATHER REPORTS
MOUNTAINCALL - 0898 500 442
Issued by Glasgow Met. Office, this is a service for hill-walkers, climbers and skiers which details expected conditions in the various hill-walking areas for the next twelve hours. It's usually more accurate than TV or radio weather forecasts, because instead of lumping together all points north of Glasgow, it recognises that conditions vary from one range of hills to another.

CLIMB LINE.   0898 654 668 (East Highlands).
0898 654 669 (West Highlands)   Give avalanche reports.
WEATHERLINE: Aberdeen & Grampian - (0224) 8091
SCOTLAND'S WEATHER - 0898 654 600
WEATHERCALL: West Central Scotland - 0898 500 421
East Central Scotland - 0898 500 423
Grampian & East Highlands - 0898 500 424
N.W. Scotland - 0898 500 425
ROAD LINE (Weather for motorists)
Highland 0898 654 610

Note: This information was correct at the time of going to press. Information numbers do change from time to time. A card detailing some of the '0898' services can be obtained by telephoning 01-895 8983.

Big Wullie in his Go-Anywhere Suzuki

ON THE ROAD

It is a sad fact that snow has the awkward habit of falling not only on the pistes but on the access roads as well. The ski resort managers, who get the blame for most things, have not yet come up with a way of preventing this, but both they and the Council snowclearers invest an enormous amount of time, money and effort in getting rid of the end result.

Contrary to popular belief, the chairlift companies are actually anxious to get the skiers up the hill so that they can start taking their money off them, but certain combinations of geography and weather conspire to make it a gargantuan task.

In the dark and chilly hours while skiers are still snoring the snow-clearing squads go to work, quite often wreaking small but largely unappreciated miracles, like clearing half a mile of twenty-foot drifts by 10am (Cairngorm 1988), but if the wind is drifting the snow in as fast as it can be cleared, then even Big Wullie in his Go-Anywhere Suzuki will get no skiing until it drops. He and those like him who drive round the snow gates 'tae ha'e a wee crack at it,' seriously impede the whole clearance operation and deserve all they get — half a ton of snow on the roof and some neat holes in the bodywork caused by stones thrown from the snowcutter, most likely.

ON BEING PREPARED

More often than not, however, the ploughs and blowers finally win and the police allow the impatient horde through the snow gates. All then goes well until the inevitable moment when someone runs out of traction on the hill. Everything slides to a halt, with or without impact, and no-one can get going again.

This is the point where those who have spent their hard-earned cash on four-wheel drive, snow chains, snow clamps or even just studded tyres, will win out, provided there's enough space to get past. Wearing the obligatory supercilious smile they steam

Lingerie salesman who kept himself alive.......

triumphantly by, leaving the luckless one to burn his way through to the tarmac. If, however, Baldy Tyres has succeeded in blocking the road completely (he's guaranteed not to have brought a shovel, incidentally), he will be very lucky not to have his personal wellbeing seriously threatened. Let no man stand between a skier and his snow.

The motoring organisations recommend not only getting your car properly shod for winter but that you should always carry basic items like a shovel, a thermos or equipment for making hot drinks, plus food and a sleeping bag. A vehicle rapidly becomes like a refrigerator in wintry conditions, and some of us still cherish memories of the lingerie salesman who kept himself alive in The Big Blizzard of '78 by decking himself out in his entire stock of ladies' tights.

One handy little trick if you stop and can't get going again is to use the mats out of the footwells to shove under the driving wheels. Make a little hole in each mat and tie it to the bumper with a piece of strong twine or rope. When you reach flat ground you can pause to remove them.

If you do become thoroughly stuck, try to push the car to where it won't be flattened by the next snowplough along, or if this is impossible it's imperative to mark it, e.g. by tying dad's boxer shorts to the aerial. You can run the engine to keep warm but it's

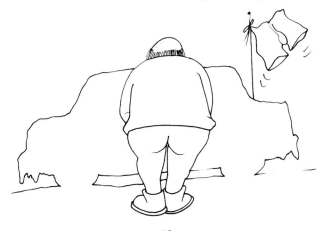

vital to check regularly that the exhaust pipe hasn't become blocked with snow; asphyxiation by exhaust fumes is an insidious and very real danger. Never go to sleep with the engine running; the recommended maximum time is to run it for ten minutes in any hour, in case there are leaks into the passenger compartment, and check the exhaust is still clear before starting it again.

To minimise your chances of having to cope with such dramas you can check the road situation before you set out, either with the Traveline numbers below or the nearest Police office. As with the ski reports, however, you should try to get the most up-to-date information possible, and bear in mind that conditions are constantly changing.

Some of the deadliest conditions on ski roads arise when the temperature suddenly drops below freezing and a wet road instantly becomes a skating rink. Braking or turning sharply on such a surface can be disastrous, and the obvious but widely-ignored rule is to keep the speed down. The Ski Hog, in his headlong rush to pick up half a dozen places in the car park, is a menace at all times but is odds-on favourite to be the first one caught out by the unexpected. Unfortunately, when he eventually does buy his ticket to the Great White Piste in the skies, he may take one or two poor innocent souls with him.

THE ROAD REPORTS

ROAD LINE (Weather for motorists)
Highland 0898 654 610
Grampian   0898 654 620
Tayside, Lothian & Border   0898 654 630
Argyll, Strathclyde & SW Scotland   0898 654 640
ABERDEEN MET. OFFICE TRAVELINE - (0224) 722334
WHOLE OF SCOTLAND - 041-246 8021

CHAPTER TWO

INTO THE FRAY
THE CAR PARK

Skiing in Scotland is expanding at such a phenomenal rate that peak-season parking is becoming a major problem at the downhill ski areas. Roadside parking is not permitted by the police, for obvious safety reasons, and it is quite simply the case on busy days that latecomers will be turned away. So it is worth bearing in mind that anyone who makes a late decision to go skiing because it happens to be a sunny day is likely to be one of hundreds, or even thousands, with the same idea. At times some of these are inevitably going to be disappointed, so taking along your hillwalking gear as well could be a wise precaution to avoid the total waste of a day.

Ski area car parks are places of constant activity and incident. Many drivers, assuming that the car park attendant has been selected on the basis of his athletic prowess, feel compelled to test his reflexes and are amazed at his ability to leap from under their front wheels with precision timing, never ceasing to wave his arms about and swear.

Others, doubtless fluorescent-green colour-blind, pretend not to see him at all and just leave the car where it stalls, which is invariably where it will get in everyone's way, and end up being shifted by the snowplough. Yet others fail to comprehend that the whole point of parking in straight lines is so that the maximum number of people can get safely in and out to enjoy their skiing, and that individuality is counterproductive to this aim.

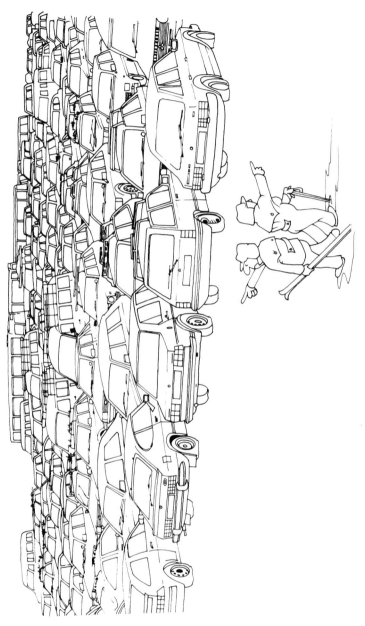

Parking a major problem

A mysterious phenomenon in the car parks, particularly at Cairngorm, is the sudden appearance of large boulders foreign to the local geology. It has now been deduced that these are imported by drivers who suffer nightmares about having the handbrake freeze up, or perhaps do not even possess handbrakes. Unfortunately, when they depart they often neglect to pick up their rocks. When buried under the next snowfall, these can have disastrous effects on snow-clearing machinery, not to mention the nerves and dental equipment of the drivers. So please, if you must bring a pet rock, do try and remember to take it home with you.

Once the business of juxtaposing cars is over, everyone has told everyone else that their lights are still on, and the driver has gone off to have a quiet word with the pratt who cut him up on the access road, the rest of the party start getting the skis out and the boots on. This is a tricky business because everyone else is also in a tearing hurry to get in their first queue of the day and repeated blows to the backside from neighbouring car doors can erode the atmosphere of bonhomie just a little. Wiser souls sit and have a cup of coffee whilst the melee sorts itself out, knowing that this is the prime time for playing 'spot-the-poseur'.

DRESSED FOR THE HILL OR DRESSED TO KILL?

In a skier's world a man is judged not by his *wedeln* but by his apparel. For those to whom sport is merely incidental to the thrill of indulging the inner peacock, skiing is the perfect choice.

The modern ski shop, rioting with pinks, limes, crimsons, turquoises, saffrons and eye-blasting fluorescents, strongly resembles an overstuffed aviary for exotic birds, right down to the elegant creatures strutting in front of the mirrors. Nevertheless, however garish its hue, the modern skisuit does a very good job of insulating its wearer against the elements, and elements are what we get plenty of in Scotland.

Waterproofing is one of the most desirable qualities to go for,

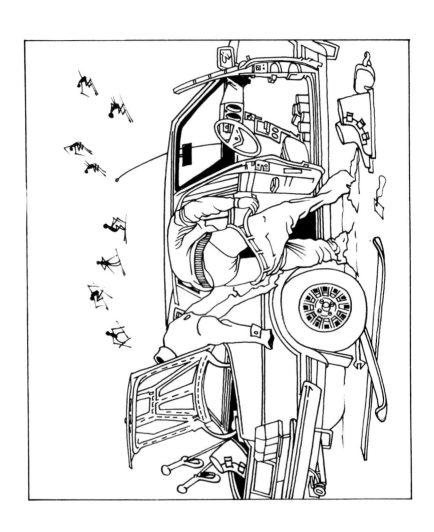

18

since what falls as dry, delightful powder in the Alps comes down in an altogether soggier form here.   Skiers rarely admit to falling — just taking a breather or stopped to look at the view are among the commoner euphemisms — but all of us do cut grooves in the snow sometimes, and this is when the cheaper fashion-before-function fabrics can actually be heard slurping up the moisture.   Combining a soggy skisuit with a chilly north-westerly makes for a really miserable day, so make sure the garments you buy are actually intended for skiing.

Scotland, however, provides a tough testing ground for any skisuit.   Even the most expensive modern fibres have difficulty in resisting a truly foul day here; sooner or later the water may well work its way through, so a change of clothing in the car or bus is essential.

Insulation and draughtproofing are vital, with cuffs, collars and zips being the most vulnerable spots.   One-piece suits generally score well for warmth, and are great for most Scottish skiing, provided they're loose enough for adding and subtracting layers underneath.   However, a closely-guarded secret is that even here there are a surprising number of warm, sunny days, and these, together with the inevitable effects of the ill-advised consumption of too much beer, can be among the few occasions when the one-piecer curses his or her choice of garb.

The key to warmth is, however, what you wear underneath, and there is no doubt that for next to the skin, polypropylene fabric is by far the best, since it wicks moisture away into the outer layers, a major factor in keeping warm for those engaged in potentially sweaty pursuits.   For insulation, lots of thin layers are far more effective at trapping warm air than one or two thick ones, and also make heat-control easier.

Good quality gloves are an excellent investment and it's wise to keep a dry pair with you or in the car, since cold extremities are the cause of much misery.   Some people swear by pure silk inner gloves, but real chilblain sufferers should be cheered by the news

Elegant creatures strutting.....

that it is now possible to buy disposable handwarmer packs in most ski equipment shops. These provide heat for several hours, and are especially useful for children, in whom cold hands are usually the first symptom of the 'whining-little-wimp' syndrome so familiar to skiing parents.

A hat is important for cold days, since much of the body's heat is lost through the head, and securely-fitting glacier specs on a cord or goggles with tinted lenses provide good eye protection and greatly improve visibility in mist. Anti-fog goggles are especially worth-while, since bad-visibility days often provide perfect climatic conditions for misting up.

There is a wide choice of containers available for carrying the items you need, whether it's full survival gear and food for a long tour or just little essentials like lip salve and a litre of Bell's.

A wide choice of containers

21

Waistbags, known universally as bumbags, are compact and can be worn cross-wise if preferred, while backpacks of all sizes should be carefully chosen for comfort rather than style. The 'Look!-I'm-being-attacked-by-a-koala-bear' fad is a little passe now and always did look silly on strapping six-footers anyway. A waist strap stops the pack from swaying about, but should always be released if you're crossing a potential avalanche slope, and if you intend to do any touring or ski mountaineering, make sure that the ski and ice-axe straps are strong and sensibly positioned.

People who ski in denim jeans fall into two distinct categories: fools or experts. The latter, few and far between, are instantly recognisable by the way they ski, and of course they never fall over. The former are much more numerous, are instantly recognisable by their wet legs and are known to succumb rapidly to hypothermia.

People who ski in denim jeans

GETTING EQUIPPED

Every winter the newspaper classified columns sprout an array of ads. which all tell the same story. 'Ski Boots - latest model - hardly worn' or, as appeared quite recently, 'Skis and sticks, suit six foot man in good condition'. The moral of all these ads should be obvious, but unfortunately it's horribly easy to land yourself with the wrong skis or boots, and it's a prime way to lose both money and confidence. There is now such a glut of secondhand skiing equipment on the market that you'll be lucky to get a reasonable sum however good the condition. So if you're just starting out, hire your equipment until you're hooked.

In the case of buying boots, if you're not absolutely sure they're going to be comfortable after a few hours' wear, ask the shop if you can take them on approval and wear them indoors (on carpets only) for a day or so. If they're reluctant to agree to this, then find out what they're prepared to do if you and your boots don't get on. Many manufacturers' reps. do regular rounds of the bigger ski shops and undertake troubleshooting for fitting problems, a service worth asking about.

If you're buying skis, ask the advice of more experienced skiers by all means, but don't assume that what they would buy for themselves is going to be right for you. Too many people go for high-performance skis thinking they'll soon 'grow into' them and thus improve their skiing. What usually happens is that they find they can't control them, and far from improving, their performance deteriorates rapidly. Skis that run too fast are a danger to everyone, not just their owner.

Carrying four or five pairs of skis in a fully-laden car can be uncomfortable, to say the least, and there are many ski racks on the market and available for hire. The lockable rack is particularly recommended for security and peace of mind, since ski thefts are on the increase, principally at Aviemore and Glenshee. It has even been known for skis to be stolen off the roofrack of a car whilst the owners were sitting lunching inside, and thefts from outside the cafes and toilets are all too common. There is a type of ski pole available which incorporates a telescopic ski lock and is probably the neatest way of solving the security problem, but an ordinary bicycle lock can be adapted to lock skis to the racks provided.

Ultra-violet property-marking kits are widely available, but in the case of skis prominent marks e.g. your postcode, or garish, devaluing stickers, are more likely to deter the prospective thief.

Fibreglass roof boxes are becoming increasingly popular because they protect valuable gear from the elements, and indeed are useful year round. They can, however, be difficult to pack and unpack if you're lacking in inches or you have a tall vehicle.

Overheard in ski club hut: *'It wasn't until we got to the funeral that I remembered I still had it on the roof. We got a few dirty looks, I can tell you!'*

HIRING SKIS

Most ski schools operate a hire service, as do many of the large ski shops in towns and cities. Closer to the slopes you will find a good number of places to hire equipment, but at peak times and busy weekends it is advisable to book in advance if possible, particularly if you may arrive late.

If you're planning several days' skiing, you may be able to make considerable savings by booking a ski hire package in advance. Most hotels, guest houses and self-catering operaters will happily arrange this. Those who hire by the day will need to leave some kind of deposit, e.g. driving licence or bank card, so remember to take something suitable along.

The majority of hire shops try hard to match the right skis to their customers, and many have experienced skiers on their staff. However, there are just a few cowboys about, so conduct a few basic checks before accepting skis.

Make sure the metal edges aren't proud of the soles and that there is still a reasonably flat bed of plastic left between them. For beginners, ultra-sharp edges can be more of a liability than an asset, except on the very iciest days, but if they really are hopelessly rounded then ask for a better pair. Never forget to ask how to release and reset the binding yourself: it's amazing how many people have problems with this when they fall and it's especially important for children to know how to get a ski off if it's firmly stuck in the snow.

Boots have come a long way in recent years; it's the feet that cause the problems! If possible try several different makes, ensuring that your heel is well back and your foot held firmly without being in a python-like embrace. Thin socks are best for a good fit, since the boot's own padding insulates your feet.

Some places also hire ski clothing, a great idea for last-minute impulses ('Let's have a go at skiing, darling — it looks so easy!'), or if you suspect you may not be totally smitten by the sport.

Know how to get a ski off if its firmly stuck in the snow

25

SKI HIRE ESTABLISHMENTS
NEAR THE SLOPES

AVIEMORE

Cairngorm Day Lodge, Cairngorm, Inverness-shire PH22 1RB
Tel. 0479 86 261/2/3

Ellis Brigham Mountain Sports, 9/10 Grampian Rd, Aviemore,
PH22 1RH
Tel. 0479 810175

Kinchyle House Ski Hire, Carrbridge PH23 3AA
Tel. 0479 84 243

The Shop, Glenmore, Aviemore PH22 1QU
Tel. 0479 86 253

Ski Road Skis, Inverdruie, Aviemore PH22 1QH
Tel. 0479 810922

Sports Hire, Nethybridge, Inverness-shire
Tel. 0479 82 333

GLENCOE & FORT WILLIAM AREA:

Glencoe Ski School, White Corries, Glencoe

Contact: Mr. Williams, Carnoch Hs., Glencoe PA39 4HS
Tel. 085 52 350

Nevisport, High Street, Fort William

GLENSHEE AREA:
The Angus Ski Hire, Balmoral Road, Blairgowrie
Tel. 0250 2455
Braemar Ski School, Cul-de-Zak, Aboyne, Aberdeenshire AB3
5JF
Tel. 0339 2565
Cairdsport, Spittal of Glenshee, Glenshee
Tel. 0250 85216
(May - Nov. - contact Cairdsport Aviemore.   Tel. 0479 810296)
Cairnwell Ski School, Cairnwell, by Braemar
Tel. 03383 331
Cally Ski Hire, Bridge of Cally, Perthshire
Tel. 0250 086 231
Glenshee Chairlift Co Ltd., Cairnwell, By Braemar
Tel. 03383 325
Excel Sports, Blairgowrie, Perthshire
Tel. 0250 3859
THE LECHT AREA
Candacraig, Candacraig Gardens, Strathdon, Aberdeenshire
Tel. 097 52 226
Goodbrand Skis, Corgarff, Aberdeenshire
Tel. 097 54 233
Hillcraft, 73 Main Street, Tomintoul
Tel. 097 52 207
The Lecht Ski Centre, Corgarff, Strathdon, Aberdeenshire
Tel. 09754 240
White Mountain Ski Hire, Gordon Arms Hotel, Tomintoul
Tel. 08074 206

For carrying, skis should be clipped together by the brakes or with special clips, then placed over the shoulder, tips forward. Watch out for those around you, both when hoisting your skis onto your shoulder and while carrying — never swing round suddenly; unpleasant head and facial injuries sustained in this way are quite common.

When leaving skis outside a cafe or ticket office, always stand them upright so that no-one will fall over them — people never look where they're going in ski resorts because there are so many interesting sights to ogle.

In the event that you do inadvertently scalp someone, or have a bad accident, or get your skis stolen, it is worth taking out insurance over and above the rescue cover you get when you buy your ticket. Most household policies can have a section added to them for this purpose, and there are also a number of excellent specially-tailored policies available through certain ski clubs and insurance brokers.

Always ski in control

CHAPTER THREE

'READY TO ROLL'

INSTRUCTION MATTERS

Formal ski instruction began in Scotland during the Second World War, when troops were trained in mountain warfare in the Cairngorms. In 1948, however, a ski school for pure pleasure seekers was started by Captain Bill Bracken, on a hill near Drumochter, which soon became known as The Brackenalp. In Glencoe, Frith Finlayson spearheaded a move towards more formal teaching methods, and in 1955 Karl Fuchs imported Austrian teaching techniques when he opened his ski school in Carrbridge.

Frith, in the meantime, was on an instructors' course in Switzerland, and in 1961 received his Ski School Director's Certificate. He was then instrumental in the setting up of the British Association of Professional Ski Instructors, which was to radically improve the standard of teaching in Scotland and today trains instructors to internationally recognised standards. BASI qualified instructors wear the distinctive circular BASI badge on their jackets.

Skiing, however easy the experts make it look, does not come naturally. The first time you put on a pair of skis, you move around with all the grace of a duck on a frozen pond, and anyone who expects to ski like Martin Bell after three or four days is in for a big disappointment. Unrealistic expectations are the major cause of people dropping out of skiing.

Basi-Qualified Instructors wear distinctive circular badges

What can make it fun instead of frustration is taking lessons from a good instructor. You spend far less time lying in the snow, and you won't be starting off with bad habits which can be very hard to eradicate later. You'll also find yourself tackling slopes and manoeuvres you wouldn't contemplate on your own, and learning your way around the pistes, so that you can decide where you enjoy skiing most.

At weekends and peak times the ski schools are very busy, so advance booking is advisable. Tell them as accurately as possible the standard you've reached so they can put you in the class which best suits your needs. Many schools also hire out equipment as part of a package with lessons, which may well work out cheaper than hiring elsewhere.

Tell them as accurately as possible the standard you have reached

A source of immense irritation to every ski school is the person who books and then doesn't turn up, or who rolls up late. This keeps the whole class hanging about and messes up the rota for the rest of the day. If you're held up on the road, a quick phone call will be much appreciated.

For your first few lessons, it's particularly important to wear clothing which will not only keep you warm when standing about waiting for your turn, but will also keep you dry. The nursery slopes, often being lower down the mountain, will tend to have wetter snow than higher up. Beginners do tend to embrace the piste quite a lot, and after one or two floundering episodes, ordinary jeans or trousers are soaked through and incredibly uncomfortable. It's an excellent idea to hire a decent suit until you decide whether skiing is for you.

When hiring equipment before a lesson, leave plenty of time so that you can make sure you're well fitted and that you know how to get in and out of the bindings. Having to wait in a cold wind while someone fiddles about with their bindings is an annoying waste of time for everyone in the class. The first two or three hours of the morning are the peak time for hiring, so you should allow plenty of queueing time.

If you're trying Nordic skiing for the first time, it is well worth taking some instruction. The right technique has to be mastered before you command that apparently effortless gliding motion, and it is also possible to get tuition in telemarking and parallel skiing. For those who want to steal a march on the snow, an artificial course has been constructed at Glenisla, where instruction is available year-round.

SKI SCHOOLS

AVIEMORE AREA
Badenoch Ski School, 26 High Street, Kingussie, Inverness-shire
PH21 1HR
Tel: 054 02 228
Cairdsport Aviemore Ski School, Aviemore, Inverness-shire
PH22 1PL
Tel: 0479 810 310, Fax: 0479 8106 89
Carrbridge Ski School, Carrbridge, Inverness-shire PH23 3AS
Tel. 0479 84 246
D'Ecosse Ski Sports Ltd., Aviemore, Inverness-shire PH22 1RN
Tel. 0479 810285
Highland Guides Nordic Ski School, Aviemore, Inverness-shire
PH22 1QH
Tel: 0479 810729
Newtonmore Ski School, Main Street, Newtonmore, Inverness-
shire PH20 1DA
Tel. 05403 433/447
Nethybridge Ski School, Nethybridge PH25 3ED
Tel. 0479 82333
Red Mac Ski School, 115 Grampian Road, Aviemore PH22 1RH
Tel. 0479 811166
Scottish Norwegian Ski School, Aviemore PH22 1PD Tel. 0479
810656

GLENSHEE AREA
Action Holidays, Blackwater, Glenshee PH10 6JY
Tel. 0250 4574
Cairnwell Ski School Ltd., By Braemar, Aberdeenshire AB3 5XS
Tel. 03383 331

Glenshee Ski School, Cairdsport, Spittal of Glenshee, By Blairgowrie, Perthshire PH10 7QE.
Tel. 0250 85 216 (0479 810 310 out of season)
Highland Adventure Nordic Ski School, Knockshannoch, Glenisla, By Alyth, Perthshire PH11 8PE
Tel. 0575 82 238
Ski Clinix, Cairnwell Ski School
Tel. 03383 331

GLENCOE
Glencoe Ski School, Carnoch House, Glencoe, Argyll PA39 4HS
Tel. 08552 350

THE LECHT

Battlehill Ski Centre, Battlehill Hotel, Huntly, Aberdeenshire AB5 5HX
Tel. 0466 2734
Lecht Ski School, Corgarff, Strathdon, Aberdeenshire AB3 8YP
Tel. (097 54) 240/242
Lonach Ski School, 4 Candacraig Square, Strathdon, Aberdeenshire
Tel. 097 52 207
White Mountain Ski School, Grantown-on-Spey, Aberdeenshire
Tel. 0479 2204

OUTDOOR CENTRES OFFERING INSTRUCTION/HIRE/ACCOMMODATION PACKAGES

Abernethy Outdoor Centre, Nethybridge, Inverness-shire PH25 3ED (Downhill & Nordic)
Tel. 0479 82 279
Ardeonaig Outdoor Centre, Nr. Killin, Perthshire FK21 8SY (Nordic)
Tel. 0567 2523

Ballindalloch Hostel — see under Insh Hall, below

Battlehill Ski Centre, Huntly, Aberdeenshire AB5 5HX (Downhill & Nordic)
Tel. 0466 2734

Braemar Youth Hostel, SYHA, 161 Warrender Park Road, Edinburgh EH9 1EQ (Downhill & Nordic)
Tel. 031 229 8660

Craigower Lodge, Golf Course Road, Newtonmore, Inverness-shire PH20 1AT (Downhill & Nordic)
Tel. 05403 319

Insh Hall Ski Lodge, Kincraig, Kingussie PH21 1NU (Downhill & Nordic)
Tel. 05404 272

Loch Morlich Youth Hostel — book with SYHA, see Loch Morlich details (Downhill & Nordic)

Ski Backcountry, Maelstrom, Insh, Kingussie, Inverness-shire (Nordic Touring)
Tel. 05402 805

PRE-SKI PREPARATION

Until the seventies, the hills were alive to the sound of breaking limbs, notably tibias and femurs. In the last fifteen years, however, there has been an enormous reduction in fractures from skiing accidents and these days, thanks to the advances in boot and binding technology, it's the muscles, ligaments and tendons that are taking the punishment. A large number of such injuries inevitably crop up at the beginning of the season.

The reason for this is the average skier's conviction that (a) he is indestructible,(b) his skis and bindings look after themselves, and (c) his innate athleticism is all the preparation he needs for skiing.

The truth of the matter is that, however fit you may be (or think you are) already, skiing uses muscles you didn't know you had, and will soon wish you hadn't. Even just a bad strain can keep you off skiing (and other things) for weeks, so pre-ski preparation means more than a quick coat of wax on the old skis. Both you and your skis need to be got in shape for the season and for the skis the process will be quicker and easier.

Swimming, running, aerobics etc. are excellent for general cardio-vascular fitness, which helps you get a lot more out of your skiing, but to avoid injury or strains you require more specific exercises for the legs, knees, thighs and abdominal muscles.

Many of the glossy new ski technique books have excellent sections on the best exercises to do, and these can be undertaken either at home or in the local gym. Many gyms and fitness centres have staff who will work out a programme for you which is aimed at strengthening these specific areas, but try and ensure that they cover the full range you need.

A recent innovation in many gyms is that new instrument of torture, the ski trainer. This consists of a free-spinning turntable which can be moved from side to side on a platform, plus spring-mounted poles for timing and balance. Although this machine looks and feels lethal on the first encounter, it actually takes very little time to master the brute and even less to deduce, from the protesting leg muscles, that it must be doing some good.

The Thomas Cook Trainer, a rolling slope, is found in many larger ski stores around the country, where it is possible to book instruction packages — ideal for pre-holiday training.

Probably the best way to prepare for the season, however, is to go to a dry slope. For experienced skiers it's perfect for re-educating the muscles, while for beginners a regular brush with the bristles is actually a very good way to learn to ski, since you can do it in the good weather and forgo the teeth-chattering pleasure of standing for hours in wind and storm watching your classmates thrashing about in the snow. It's also supposed to be good for the technique, which actually means that it's so unforgiving that when you finally get onto the snow you find you can ski rather well after all.

No special equipment is needed for dry slope skiing other than a pair of robust mitts, preferably not a pair you care too much about, and equally robust trousers and anorak. Fingers and thumbs tend to be somewhat traumatised by falls on latticed matting and need plenty of protection.

If you have your own boots it's fine to take them along but don't use your own skis unless you're prepared to write them off for snow use — the artificial surface is very hard on them. Practically all the slopes have good hire facilities, but it's wise to telephone before going along: some slopes are open only for certain months of the year.

Dry slope skiing should not be spurned by Nordic enthusiasts as a way of getting fit. Although it does not use quite the same muscles, and comes second best to roller skiing as specific preparation, it is widely regarded as being a lot better than nothing, and some slopes now offer Nordic instruction. Some slopes also provide facilities and instruction for disabled skiers.

DRY SKI SLOPES IN SCOTLAND
(Length of slope in brackets — in metres)
Ancrum Outdoor Education Resource Centre, 10 Ancrum Road, Dundee
Tel. 0382 60719. 60m.
Alford Dry Ski Slope, Greystone Road, Alford, Aberdeenshire
Tel. 0336 2251
Bearsden Ski Club, The Mound, Bearsden, Glasgow
Tel. 041 942 2933
Drambuie Ski Slope, Aviemore Centre, Aviemore
Tel. 0479 810310. (50m.)
Fife Institute of P & RE, Viewfield Road, Glenrothes
Tel. 0592 771770. (35m.)
Firpark Ski Centre, Tillicoultry, Clackmannanshire
Tel. 0259 51772
Glasgow Ski Centre, Bellahouston Park, 16 Drumbreck Road, Glasgow
Tel. 041-427 4991. (80m.)

Hillend Ski Centre, Biggar Road, Edinburgh
Tel. 031 445 4433. (400m.)
Irvine Valley Ski Slope, High Street, Kilmarnock
Tel. 0560 22320
Kaimhill Ski Slope, Kaimhill Playfield, Garth Dee Road, Bridge of Dee, Aberdeen
Tel. 0224 38707. (85m.)
Loch Rannoch Hotel, Kinloch Rannoch, by Pitlochry
Tel. 08822 201, Extension 109. (70m.)
Polmonthill Ski Centre, Polmont, Stirlingshire
Tel. 0324 711660. (100m.)
Royal Marines Condor Camp, Arbroath
Tel. 0241 72201. (105m.) Mainly for Service personnel; can be booked by ski clubs.
Stoneywood Outdoor Education Centre Ski Slope, 105 Stoneywood Road, Bucksburn, Aberdeen
Tel. 0224 712462. (30m.)

SKI MAINTENANCE

The notion that skis thrive on neglect seems to be widespread, but come the first icy morning there is always a stampede to the repair shop to get the edges sharpened.

Edges, whilst indispensable, are only part of the ski's ability to help you ski well. In Scottish skiing, the soles in particular are subject to special kinds of abuse because of our enthusiasm for tackling rocks, heather, peatbogs, snowfences etc., and not all of us are rich enough to afford a new pair every season.

Having your skis serviced by a reputable ski technician is a very worthwhile move, and should ideally be done at the end of each season. Left with an encrustation of peat and road salt, they can only deteriorate, and if it turns out that you have ruined them beyond repair, it gives you time to save up for replacements. You should also get the bindings checked, and enquire about the best way to store them.

Professional ski servicing is quite expensive, and quickly mounts up if you are skiing every weekend throughout the season. This is when it pays to learn how to do at least part of your ski maintenance yourself.

For a week or two you may get away with just filling up the holes with wax, but before long the ever-multiplying gouges will need more radical doctoring.

If you are good at learning from books, scout around the local library for a general ski book which includes a section on P-Texing, hot waxing and sharpening. Data Ski Care of Aberdeen supply a comprehensive range of waxing and maintenance equipment, while a leaflet 'Ski Servicing Made Easy' is available from another Scottish-based company, Kandie Imports, who also supply a large range of maintenance tools and materials. (See appendix for both addresses.)

Many dry ski slopes do courses which include ski maintenance, or would perhaps be willing to give you some tuition if you booked a small group in. Ski Shows almost always have servicing exhibits and ski clubs also often run maintenance evenings.

Materials are available from most ski shops and by mail order. A note about files, though: very few people are skilled enough to get the edges precisely right with a flat file, and often do more harm than good. In fact, the edges on some new skis could never be properly sharpened this way because of their angles. Even right-angle files have to be handled carefully, so ideally take expert advice before you attack your best skis.

Having honed both your skis and your body to a state of stunning perfection, don't forget that muscles, like car engines, need to warm up before they're ready to give of their best. Those who leap, gibbering with excitement, straight from the car to the chairlift and then plunge down the black run for their first buzz of the day are asking for it — and usually get it sooner or later, in the form of pulled ligaments and damaged tendons at the very least. If you find limbering-up exercises embarrassing (they are in fact totally accepted for other sports — why not skiing?) then just take it easy until you're firing on all cylinders.

And at the end of the day, when the blood is up and the spirit is still willing, it pays to be able to recognise when the body is weakening. Late afternoon is the time when most accidents occur.

You should never take that 'one last run'. That's when you'll do yourself an injury. Brian Cameron, B.A.S.I. Ski Instructor.

CHAPTER FOUR

UPLIFTING THOUGHTS

JUST THE TICKET

All the Scottish chairlift companies now use tickets, having phased out the old punchcards. For the ultra-keen, a season ticket is usually good value, particularly when bought at the cheap rate in autumn, and there are also special deals for families, plus various combinations of weekly tickets. The chairlift companies issue an up-to-date list of their ticket prices every autumn and will send it on request.

CAIRNGORM:The Ticket Office, Cairngorm Chairlift Co. Aviemore Tel. (0479) 86261
GLENSHEE: Glenshee Chairlift Company, Cairnwell Mountain, By Braemar, Aberdeen AB3 5XU Tel. (03383) 320
GLENCOE: White Corries Ltd., Main Office, Walled Garden House, Ballachulish PA39 4HT Tel. 08556 226
LECHT: The Lecht Ski Co Ltd., Lecht Ski Centre, Corgarff, Aberdeenshire Tel. 09756 51440

Full Area day or half-day tickets are intended for proficient skiers who can make use of the whole ski area and all the lifts, while Limited Area tickets are ideal for the less experienced.

Once you've bought your ticket you have to pass a combined IQ and dexterity test — i.e. attaching it to your person in the correct manner. To do this you need one of those little wire triangles so often seen lying in the mud; don't forget to take one out of the box or, in the case of Cairngorm, off the rack beside the tables.

In theory it's simple: you just slip the wire through the eye of your zip, peel off the backing paper, stick half of the ticket onto the wire frame, fold the rest under and stick it to itself on the other side. See - piece of cake! What they don't tell you in the instructions is that the adhesive sticks to EVERYTHING it touches like honey to a blanket and will not, under any circumstances, come off again without self-destructing. There's no second chance if you mess it up the first time: once on, it's on for the day, the whole point being that it has be permanently attached to prevent fraud.

This means that if you decide to take off your anorak, you can't move your ticket, so if the weather looks promising it's a good idea to attach it to your sweater or your salopettes zip. On windy days (which means potentially just about any day at 3,000 feet), you can avoid the unsightly appearance of a severely-lacerated chin by not fastening your ticket to the very top of your jacket.

UPWARDLY MOBILE

Asking the lift attendant where he went to charm school does not guarantee a safe passage up the hill, particularly if yours is the fifteenth ski pole with which he's been jabbed in the groin today. In the main, they're pretty tolerant, and many are even helpful, which is quite surprising considering the amount of hassle they get from skiers.

Keeping the tows going is one of the major headaches for all the ski centres, and what the managers and operators need least of all is advice. They are frequently accosted by self-styled 'experts' offering the benefit of their wisdom, and it is not always appreciated.

An 'ex' is a has-been and a 'spurt' is a drip under pressure! — Bruce Forbes, Manager, White Corries, Glencoe.

The entire lift system has been carefully designed to get the maximum number of skiers per hour safely up the hill, and, believe it or not, mechanical failure is very rare indeed. It's estimated that more than 99% of stoppages are caused by the skiers themselves, meaning hours of frustration and lost skiing while the problems are sorted out.

CHAIRLIFTS

There are three main types of chairlift in use in Scotland: the single chair, the double forward-facing chair and the double side-facing chair. The principles for getting on and off are much the same — watch carefully what everyone else is doing and get yourself and your equipment sorted out well in advance.

If the take-off is on snow, you will be wearing your skis and should carry your poles by gripping them half way down. Stand well-balanced with your skis parallel and facing forwards, then turn and prepare to catch hold of the arm of the chair just as it scoops you up. Bend your knees and relax into the seat, then put the safety bar down if there is one. A bulky rucksack should be removed and carried on your knee, since there may not be enough room for both of you.

If you have to carry your skis and sticks up, fasten your skis together and gather the whole lot in your arms like a bundle of messages. At Glencoe you sit with them across your body and at Cairngorm you stand them on the footrest between your knees.

Never keep the wrist straps of your poles on whilst on a chair, (or any other kind of tow for that matter) because if the poles catch in anything the results can be disastrous. Also keep skis and poles up above the level of your feet, particularly at Cairngorm where sticks quite frequently get mangled on the platform when the chair goes into the top station.

Once aboard you can look at the view — scenic or human, whichever appeals most — but don't forget to watch out for the instruction boards telling you when to lift the bar and prepare to get off. If you're on foot, just stand up with your knees slightly flexed and move quickly to the side, out of the way of the chair. On snow, stand up as soon as your ski tips touch the top of the ramp, then point them straight down the slope. There's always plenty of room to slow down and stop once you're on safe snow, provided everyone has had the sense to move out of the way.

The golden rule for the tops of lifts is: once you've arrived, get the hell out of it!

WHAT TO DO WITH A POMA

This is the type of lift where you place the disc or button between your legs and allow it to push you up the hill. It looks dead easy, and so it is, as long as everyone follows a few basic rules. The trouble is, they don't, and that's how all the stoppages occur.

1) Remove your wrists from the straps of your ski sticks and grasp them half-way along. Getting a stick caught on the bars causes unpleasant injuries.

2) Wait for the green light before grabbing the front poma in the bundle. Step past the trip bar, which starts your poma off, and flex your knees ready for take-off.

3) Don't sit down on the button! The poles are spring-loaded, so all that happens is that you end up on the deck. Once you've got going, stand up straight and let it push you up the hill.

4) If you fall off, let go! This may sound like an insult to anyone's intelligence but it's astonishing how many people hang on like grim death, shedding skis and clothing as they cut a painful swathe up the hill. Just give up and try again. If by any chance your clothing gets caught, yell to someone to stop the tow. There are stop buttons on the pylons at regular intervals for just such emergencies.

5) Don't ziz-zag. This is one of the most important rules. Try to keep underneath the cable at all times, particularly if the wind or a slight slope is making everyone drift sideways. The danger is that by skiing out to the side you'll pull the cable off the pulley. When this happens the tow will be off for ages while they fix it.

6) Don't get off before the top. When you let go, the bar retracts

violently; it can easily wrap itself round a pole or the cable, which means another lengthy wait.

6) Get off where the notice tells you. If you ski on any further you'll trip the safety mechanism which stops the tow and means someone will have to come right up from the bottom to reset it. This is an irritatingly common reason for a stoppage and will drop your popularity rating among fellow skiers pretty drastically.

THE TAMING OF THE T-BAR

Although the basic principle is the same as for the poma, the T-bar, being built for two, is a far more entertaining means of transport.

You can meet all kinds of folk on a T-bar. For the Nosey Blighter, for instance, every trip is an excuse for a full-scale interrogation; by the time you get to the top he or she will know all about you, even down to the brand of socks you wear, whereas the Silent Type dries up as soon as the weather's finished with, if not before.

In between these two extremes are the characters with whom you can have some fascinating conversations about topics you never dreamed of. My own general knowledge has been memorably augmented by one man's all-too-graphic account of how it felt to fall off the Matterhorn and another's equally picturesque theories about what makes camels fart.

The curse of the slopes, however, is the T-Bore, who is delighted to have a captive audience and will have bored the pants off you before the first pylon. The art of shoving someone else off a T-bar whilst staying on yourself is well worth practising, but you should always make it look like an accident.

Staying on, in fact, can be a craft in itself and may actually rule out conversation on your part, since you could easily end up with a Boot-Hooker or a Leaner.

The Boot-Hooker has a knack of locking his boot clips in a deadly embrace with yours, whereupon you both start to lose

45

balance. Since he's used to this, and is almost certainly a T-Bore as well, he'll carry on happily chatting whilst you launch into a frantic stamp-shuffle-step routine until you free it. This is a waste of time since three seconds later they'll be welded together again: all you can do is hope they'll break it up if and when you reach the top.

The Leaner, who is sure to be a lot bigger and heavier than you are, and apparently exists on a diet of garlic and peppermints, clearly considers your role to be a supporting one. Apart from claustrophobia, suffocation and crushed ribs, your biggest worry is hitting a patch of ice, since your edges will need to support the two of you. If in spite of all your scratching and scrabbling the crunch does come, try to hold onto the bar a fraction longer than he does so that you can turn the tables and use him as a cushion.

If you're going up on your own, which can definitely be safer, do not, repeat not, put the bar between your legs. Seemingly intelligent, good-looking blokes are seen doing this every season and it makes one's eyes water to think of the possible outcome in the event of an accident.

On an equally sobering note, the most dangerous place on a T-bar is at the top, where the cardinal sin is to let go of the bar too soon. If you do this there is a strong probability that it will hit the person behind you on the head, possibly causing serious injuries.

Always decide in advance who will take care of the bar. The other person should get off first and ski well away to the side while the remaining skier keeps hold of the bar and lets the rope run right round the wheel at the top. Then let the remaining bit retract into the holder as it comes past you before letting go and quickly getting right out of the way of the next person coming up. Occasionally a bar doesn't retract fully even when you've done all the right things, so be prepared to bellow the time-honoured warning 'Mind ya heid!' if necessary. Sassenachs should memorise this phrase in advance, as waiting for a translation is not a good idea if you happen to be on the receiving end.

It's easy to overlook the fact that the tows are the most crucial element in downhill skiing and that without them we'd be back to herring-boning. Keeping them going should be the concern of everyone, skiers in particular, and not just looked on as the sole responsibility of the chairlift company.

QUEUE TIPS

Deciding where to ski is a delicate art. Even the old hands get it wrong quite often, because every piste is different in the way it holds its snow and reacts to weather conditions. An overnight blizzard or a thaw followed by a frost can transform yesterday's ego-trip mogul field into today's nightmare survival course.

The fact that there is a long queue for a particular tow might lead one to imagine that this is where the best skiing is to be had. This, known as Sheep's Law, is a dubious assumption, and reveals a basic lack of understanding of human nature.

When released from their cars, skiers tend to head straight for their favourite runs, regardless of the weather or snow conditions. Those who are new to the area or who do not yet have a favourite run then use Sheep's Law to decide where to go. Before you can say 'Please do not stand on the backs of my skis' or words to that effect, there's a queue to rival a Warsaw bakery.

It can be quite astounding how long many people are prepared to stand in a queue, often when the waiting time far exceeds that taken to ski down the run. An example of this is when, at peak times on Cairngorm, a wait of almost an hour has not been unknown on Coire Cas, while the Aonach run, just over the ridge, has been relatively quiet and in excellent condition. Patience may be a virtue but a bit of enterprise gets you a lot more skiing. (In the individual Ski Area descriptions, you'll find notes on queuing blackspots and hints for avoiding them.)

Unlike the Alps, where the fastest and fittest get to go up the tows first, regardless of when they arrived on the scene, in Scotland queueing is a revered art form.

47

The most despised creature on the slopes is the Brazen Queuehopper, easily distinguished by his brass neck and battered ski-tips, and not to be confused with lesser sub-species like the Bumbling Twit, who simply can't work out where the end of the queue is, or the Chancer, who simply doesn't care.

The Brazen Queuehopper relies for his success on speed and surprise and has perfected the knack of arriving swiftly at the front of the line whenever someone is slow to close a gap. Hardly ever is he challenged, and if he is he'll just pretend to be deaf, or protest that his Aunty's been keeping his place, or that he's Franz Klammer in disguise...by which time he's on his way up. The only way to fettle this character is to use a couple of swift stabs of your ski-poles to 'accidentally' release his bindings, then crowd him so he can't get them back on again. Apologise sweetly for your clumsiness as you push him aside.

It is advisable to refrain from practising this trick on Ski Patrols, Chairlift Company Directors and lift operators, who are allowed to jump queues. The latter can sometimes be difficult to recognise, but look for clues like unpretentious (oil-stained?) ski gear, an expression of world-weariness and vastly superior skiing ability.

The majority of queuing arguments arise when a second, third or fourth line has been formed and hordes of people, Bumbling Twits and Chancers alike, start joining onto the wrong one.

Occasionally it's difficult to decide which line is the last one, but nearly always it's marked by someone leaping up and down brandishing their poles and frantically shouting 'New queue!' If you pretend not to notice and join the old line, you'll just get squeezed out nearer the tow.

If you decide to start a new queue yourself, it pays to make an arrangement with the person on the end of the old one, so they can send new arrivals down to you. Select the largest, most aggressive-looking character you can find — it's no good picking a wimp for this.

Some groups, e.g. junior racers, have priority on certain lifts like the M1 (Cairngorm) and Cairnwell (Glenshee), and often there's a sign to this effect, so if you elect to ski on that run you just have to put up with extra-long queuing times. Priority is usually on a one-for-one basis, however, so if thirty-three gaudily-clad little brats try to push in front of you, check their credentials with the tow-operator. A be-stickered helmet is not an automatic pass to the front of every queue.

......wasn't here last season

CHAPTER FIVE

'WHAT GOES UP....'

A ski run is really a kind of survival course. Putting on a pair of skis is psychologically similar to getting behind the wheel of a car, in that it transforms the mildest, most inoffensive souls into cursing, cut-throat speed-freaks. And just as on the roads, many of the accidents which occur are a direct result of this fast-is-clever attitude.

Recently a seven year old girl had to have emergency brain surgery as a result of being knocked down by a man treating one of the intermediate pistes as a downhill course. After the collision, which was spectacular to say the least, he picked himself up, put his skis back on and skied off, not even pausing to see if she was all right.

VITAL STATISTICS — INJURIES
Records of ski injury statistics from the last twenty-three seasons have formed the basis of a fascinating and instructive study carried out by the Department of Orthopaedic Surgery at Dundee Royal Infirmary.

Based on the records of 6,923 skiers attending hospitals serving the north-east of Scotland, the most recent report shows some interesting findings. (The above figure constitutes approximately thirty per cent of all the injuries dealt with by the ski rescue services at the centres concerned — initially Cairngorm and Glenshee, now including the Lecht.) A very clear finding is that the risk of injury is most closely related to skiing experience.

For the seasons 1984 and 1985, 726 skiers presented to the hospitals in the study, and in 639 of these cases the circumstances of the injury-producing accident were recorded. Five major causes of injury were identified, 'the most common being a fall in good snow conditions due to lack of control when moving at speed or due to falls in soft snow when travelling relatively slowly.' Hazards in the terrain and collisions with other skiers, pylons, snowfences and even piste-bashers were identified as other causes. Tables detailing these findings are reproduced in the Appendix to this book.

One of the most sobering features of these findings is the type of injury most likely to be suffered by children. 'More than two-thirds of children's injuries are in the lower limb and approximately half of these are twist-related injuries to the ankle and tibia.' In adults this sort of injury has shown a marked decrease in recent years, and it is assumed that this is largely due to the improvements in ski bindings and boots. The reasons why the safety release binding seems to fail to protect younger skiers are largely spec-ulative, but may be partly because childrens' bindings tend to be less sophisticated than adults' and are less likely to have the settings checked regularly.

It is pointed out in the study that children 'tend to use equipment provided by schools, youth groups and hire shops and have little personal interest in its maintenance and adjustment.' A child who finds his bindings release too easily may try to adjust them himself and end up with too high a setting. 'Ideally children require safety bindings of modern design which are well main-tained and once adjusted to the recommended retention value require more than fingers or the edge of a coin to alter that setting.'

The fact that children, particularly young males, are more likely than adults to sustain injuries of any sort is thought to be principally due to lack of experience and ability. They also tend to ski for more hours per day, and may have less regard for their own safety than adults.

Males of all ages figure more prominently than females in the accident figures, which undoubtedly reflects their preponderance in the skiing population overall. The paper also speculates whether this is in part due 'to the individual's voluntary exposure to hazard or skiing style', doubtless a polite way of suggesting that, in general, males have a more aggressive approach to skiing and that you are less likely to be cut up and flattened by a lady skier. Shame!

Indisputable conclusions drawn by the study are that 'the probability of injury increases with the number of hours skied and the time of day. Fatigue, visibility and snow conditions are factors which vary throughout the day.'

It was noted that the average injury rates were higher at Glenshee (4.84 per thousand skier days) than at Cairngorm (1.90 per thousand skier days), but this is likely to be largely due to the fact that approximately half of all the injuries sustained on Cairngorm are vetted by the Health Centre in Aviemore village, where there are X-ray facilities. This obviously acts as a filter, so that a large percentage will not have to attend a hospital. At Glenshee, however, all injuries are sent direct to hospital, and since the methods of calculation used in the report are based on hospital casualty figures, inevitably the Glenshee figure will be higher. It is also the case that there are differences between the two resorts in the nature of the skiing population. Cairngorm, having plenty of accommodation close by, tends to attract more experienced skiers who stay in the area for one or two weeks, whereas Glenshee, having nowhere near so many beds available within easy reach of the slopes, is used more by school and youth groups and for day trips from the Central Belt, so the preponderance of young and inexperienced skiers could be expected to be considerably greater.

'Skiers from Glenshee were also more likely to identify difficulties in the terrain as the cause of their accident, and this factor is of course not unrelated to ability and experience.'

The single most significant fact to emerge from this report, however, is the one pinpointed by all the ski rescue personnel in every ski area:

SKIING OUT OF CONTROL IS THE PRIME CAUSE OF ACCIDENTS ON THE SKI SLOPES

Skiing out of control

THE QUICK AND THE DEAD

So how could the situation be improved? Skis run away with their owners for a variety of reasons: the slope is too steep, they're not putting in enough turns, they have super-fast skis which outpace their reactions, or they're taking chances just for the sake of it. In the end it all comes down to lack of technique and experience.

The only way to gain these without sooner or later ruining someone's health, not to mention your own, is to follow three basic rules:

1) SLOW DOWN — ALWAYS SKI IN CONTROL
2) SKI ACCORDING TO THE CONDITIONS and
3) WATCH OUT FOR OTHER SKIERS

Whilst it seems that the inexperienced skier is most likely to suffer injury through a fall on the piste, some of the most unpleasant accidents result from collisions. Often the worst offenders here are the so-called experts, too intent on displaying their amazing talents to make allowances for slower skiers, and matters are made worse by the inexperienced venturing onto runs they're not yet ready for, getting in the way of those for whom the piste is really intended. Nevertheless, it is always the responsibility of the faster and hopefully more skilful skier to resist the urge to show off and give a wide berth to the less competent.

Oops....Sorry!

RECIPE FOR DISASTER - SUNNYSIDE OMELETTE

Ingredients:
5 Wide-Angle-Legs Snowploughers (W.A.L.S.) intent on personal survival.
2 Going-Out-Of-Control Sillybeggars (G.O.O.C.S.) in the 'look-I'm-a-downhill-racer' position
1 Arrogant Speed Skier (A.S.S.) returning from splendid day exhibiting his good looks and incredible skills on Glas Maol.
Method
Take 3 stationary WALS, carefully position in nearest bottleneck, then set in motion without warning and quickly add 1 cursing ASS and a GOOCS.   When resulting mixture is fermenting nicely, add 2 more WALS (with a touch of the despairing screams) and top off with a final layer of GOOCS.   Sprinkle resulting shambles liberally with snow and serve on bloodwagons.

Note: suitable for any time of day but a speciality in the late afternoon.

Regional Variations: Grouse Fricassee (The Lecht), Mugs' Alley Mash (Glencoe) and Coire Casserole (Cairngorm).

Apart from the bashers and bombers, the other prime menaces on the piste include people who stop in awkward places, often near the tops of lifts, causing pile-ups, and those who suddenly start off or turn in front of you without looking behind first.   Looking in the mirror becomes a reflex when you're driving: checking behind should be just as automatic when skiing.

It is surprising how often someone skis right through the middle of a ski class or even a race.   Apart from the rudeness, it's downright dangerous.   Anyone who has watched Ski Sunday knows what speeds downhill racers reach: an unexpected arrival on the course at the wrong moment could mean a wipe-out for both parties.   If a run is cordoned off, it may be because it is considered dangerous, or because it is being used for racing.   Signs of avalanche risk or icy runs should be heeded: they are put there for the benefit of the skiers, not because the manager got out of bed on the wrong side. If you're in doubt about any run or you come across some unmarked hazard, consult the Ski Patrol.

Many of the accidents caused by inexperienced skiers could be avoided if more people took lessons before launching themselves onto the pistes. It is an extraordinary fact that anyone beginning just about any other sport for the first time takes tuition as a matter of course, but every day the ski slopes are littered with the prone forms of those who seem to think that skiing should come 'naturally'.

THE DOG HAZARD

The canine element is a far rarer but nevertheless problematic hazard on the pistes. Skiing with a dog may seem at first to be a nice idea, good for both exercising the dog and enhancing the image of the owner, but they're discouraged at most of the Scottish ski centres for a number of wholly valid reasons.

One is that there are many inexperienced skiers around who cannot stop quickly or take avoiding action when, for instance, a dog trips over a compelling smell and slams on the brakes right under their skis.

Dogs run over by skis sustain pretty unpleasant injuries like broken legs and deep lacerations, and in certain snow conditions they can also suffer badly cut-up feet when ice crystals freeze into sharp balls in their pads. Sadly several have been known to have heart attacks from the effort and stress of following their owners up lifts in heavy snow. Dogs cover many times more ground than do their owners, so a day's skiing must be incredibly exhausting for them.

Dogs are not allowed on the hill at Glencoe and The Lecht, nor are they permitted on the trails at Glenmulliach. They are also strongly disapproved of at Cairngorm.

SKIING WITH CHILDREN

Cairngorm now bans people carrying babies in backpacks from using their tows, and other centres may do likewise.   This follows two horrendous cases abroad, where one child was found to have died of exposure in a backpack and another had to have its feet amputated as a result of frostbite.   Children in backpacks have no means of stimulating their circulation by movement, and become rapidly chilled.   They are also extremely vulnerable to injury in the event of an accident, since however good a skier the parent might be there is always the very real risk of a collision with someone less competent.

Toddlers can start skiing almost as soon as they can walk, but do avoid cheap ski sets with strap-on bindings — it simply isn't worth the risk of injury.   Quite a number of ski shops and ski clubs deal in good secondhand equipment, a considerable saving when children grow so fast.   Most hire shops now stock skis and boots in very small sizes, though you may need to book them in advance at peak times.

The golden rule with the very young is to make it fun and never push them into doing things they don't want to.   An hour or two is the absolute maximum at the beginning, and even less if the weather is at all unpleasant.   Some are tougher than others, but at the first hint of mutiny, pack it in and buy them a hot chocolate. Don't worry if they're a bit wimpish at first; before long they'll be overtaking you.   At the Lecht there is a creche, and one is also planned for Aonach Mor.

The easiest way to take a young child up a tow is to relieve them of their ski poles, set them astride your leg and let them hold on to the bar.   Instruct them properly in all the do's and don'ts of tow handling (see Chapter Four) before you let them tackle pomas or T-bars on their own.

For slightly older children, ski school is ideal, since it seldom works for parents to try and instruct their own offspring. Most schools have an instructor who is especially gifted with youngsters, and they learn better in a group. (It also gives the parents an hour or two to ski together.)

Joining a ski club is often useful for a family, and some clubs have huts on the slopes where parents can take it in turn to sprog-sit. And getting involved in club races is, as outlined in Chapter Seven, the way most young racers get started, so if you want to raise a ski-prodigy, this is where to start.

Parents should take the passing on of safety advice very seriously and not just expect their children to absorb everything by observation. When they reach the 'bombing' stage they may need a good talking to about respecting other skiers, and it is an excellent idea to issue them with a helmet for their own protection, and insist they wear it.

READING THE CONDITIONS

A primary characteristic of Scottish skiing is its variety. It is rare for two days to be alike in snow and weather conditions, and even in one day you can shiver your way through a thick, damp mist in the morning, bask in hot sunshine at noon and be caught in a howling blizzard by four. The chairlift companies quite often come under fire for running lifts when conditions are bad, but it should be remembered that some people actually enjoy skiing on sheet ice in pea soup.

Probably nowhere else in the world can one experience such a miasma of snow textures and climatic variations in such a short time. The weather can come from the frozen steppes of Russia one day and the warm South Atlantic the next, making it possible in a single week to ski such assorted delights as powder, wind slab, breakable crust, sheet ice, crud, porridge, and even smooth, dry snow.

60

The annual build-up of the Scottish snowfields is an intriguing phenomenon. The first winter falls are often heavy, with storm force winds driving the snow into every leeward corrie, streambed, gully and undulation on the landscape to the depth of sometimes tens of feet. It is at this point that it is also meant to fill the gaps between the strategically-placed snowfences, but everything depends on the wind speed and direction.

Savage thaws may then follow, accompanied by heavy rain, leaving only the gulllies snow-filled. Then the skiers pray that a frosty spell will ensue in order for the base to become hardened before the whole cycle is repeated. Depression follows depression, front after front, until there is a build-up of solid granular snowfields. These, when well-established, can resist the warmth of spring up to June and beyond in certain high gullies and corries.

Settled spells of anticyclonic weather often occur in winter and spring, and influence snow conditions according to the stage of the snow/wind/thaw cycle in which they occur. Snow that falls as light, feathery crystals either melts or converts eventually into large granular crystals. Freeze/thaw conditions greatly accelerate this process, and the larger crystals of spring snow, readily allowing rain to drain away, give the excellent conditions characteristic of Scottish spring skiing. This snow is fast and non-sticking, no matter what the temperature, though with a lot of use it can turn to porridge. It is then that the classic 'Up, down' ski technique proves inadequate, and that modern techniques of continual tail-weighting and carving come into their own.

The skier who equips himself or herself, both physically and mentally, to meet these conditions holds a great advantage. Far better to wonder at and enjoy the power of the elements than to only ski the perfect days. By skiing the bad days, the good days seem even better.

'The Scots are a breed apart and the Scottish skiing industry is based on their enthusiasm. Here the lifts are modified to run under adverse conditions and they only close if there is danger to

View of a 'White-Out'

the skier or the installation....It's up to the individual to make the decision whether to ski or not.' Tom Paul, General Manager, Cairngorm.

EVACUATION PROCEDURE

When, therefore, the decision to close a ski centre is taken, you can be sure there is an extremely good reason for it. At all the centres the hill is cleared by sounding a siren; if you hear the siren you should make your way back to the car park immediately and wait inside your vehicle for the police to advise you of the evacuation procedure. It is important to do this rather than head out willy-nilly, since the access roads may be filling in fast, and it will be necessary for cars to be organised in convoys following a snowplough. Those who stay up the hill to grab a bit more skiing once the siren has sounded will soon find the lifts closing, starting with those furthest up or out.

SCOTCH MIST

Skiing in what is euphemistically termed 'low cloud' — i.e. fog — is fine as long as you enjoy surprises. When the light goes flat, all the bumps suddenly become invisible, leading to severe strain on the shock-absorbers. Those with rubber knees have a distinct advantage at such times, since they have a better chance of staying upright.

One of the most unpleasant things which can happen to you is getting overtaken by white-out conditions. Since weather in the hills changes so fast, there may be comparatively little warning that you're about to be enveloped by a shroud of total whiteness which takes away all sensation of movement. The feeling of isolation at such times is abrupt and can be quite disturbing.

'All the other skiers vanished. No sound, nothing — they just disappeared. I felt as if I was spinning round and round. I stopped and yelled to the others, but there was just the noise of the

Stop and take your skis off

wind, nothing else. It was like being dropped in a bowl of milk. I just stood there, wondering what to do. Then I saw an amazing sight — this huge boulder came hurtling up the hill, right past me at a rate of knots. Even then, it must've taken me a good ten seconds to realise I was the one that was moving. A few seconds more and I'd have been over the edge'. Unknown skier recounting the day's adventures in pub.

On a run which you know well and which is free of major hazards, it may be possible to snowplough gently down until you find a recognisable landmark like a snowfence. When you find a fence, stay inside it — it might be the outer boundary. Keep stopping to listen for the sound of tows or other skiers, but don't assume others know where they're going. In the days before Glenshee was so well fenced, large parties of skiers on their way to Butcharts from Carn Aosda often trustingly followed each other on unscheduled tours over the back to Loch Vrotachan and had to be fetched back in droves.

If you get really disorientated in a white-out it's best to stop and take your skis off before you find the quick way over a cornice. Once your feet are in contact with *terra firma* it's easier to decide which way is down, and to follow it at a safe pace.

One possible ruse if you suspect there may be a precipice below you is to make a snowball and roll it down the slope, marking the point where it goes out of sight. Sideslip cautiously to just above that point and roll another snowball. This is fine for discovering a sheer drop straight down, but bear in mind that an overhanging cornice might bear your snowball's weight but not yours.

Never ski alone off-piste. If you injure yourself or get caught in an avalanche and no-one knows about it, you're in real trouble.

Provided you have stayed within the snow fences and markers in the main downhill centres, becoming lost on the hill should be no great problem provided you keep your head. Finding the line of a burn and following it downwards is the best plan, as sooner or later it will bring you out onto a road. If you think you may have strayed over the back markers you should follow the most logical route, i.e. downhill along the burn line, as that is where rescuers will look for you first.

If the worst comes to the worst and you decide to abandon your skis because it is safer on foot, stick them upright in the snow so that they can be more easily seen by rescuers or recovered later. Skis laid flat on the snow get rapidly drifted over and may not be seen again until the spring. The decision to abandon any item of equipment should not be taken lightly. Skis can be used to dig a snow hole or improvise a stretcher if necessary.

Cross-country skiers who venture into the mountains should always carry survival equipment and be totally sure of their navigational skills. They should learn as much as possible about the symptoms of hypothermia, which is the insidious killer and can be hard to spot since it creeps up on you gradually, when the core temperature of the body falls more than about six degrees below normal. Symptoms include increasing tiredness, apathy, clumsiness and irritability. Prevention, with plenty of thin layers of thermally efficient clothing and a specialised wind and waterproof outer garment, is far better than cure. This involves getting the subject out of the wind immediately and into some kind of shelter, then administering hot drinks and high-calorie food and finally deciding on evacuation procedure.

Even for the experienced routefinder, navigating on skis is very much more difficult than on foot because seeking out the best snow means you rarely proceed in a straight line, and having to make repeated turns affects your judgement of distance. If there is any chance at all of being caught out overnight then bivi. equipment, plenty of food and a folding snow shovel should be included. And please, if you leave your vehicle in a ski centre car park, leave a route card with the police or ski patrol giving your approximate route and when you expect to return. This is especially important if you plan to be away overnight, since an unclaimed car at the end of the day could cause a full-scale alert.

If you leave a car in a lay-by in a remote spot, it is also a good idea to leave a route card inside, so that if the police should become concerned they can establish whether or not there is likely to be a problem.

GETTING CARRIED AWAY

Testing the efficiency of the ski rescue service is something every skier confidently expects never to have to do, but each year many are proved wrong. The cost of ski rescue insurance is now included in the ticket price in all the downhill ski areas, and it's clear from the way they ski that some people are determined to get their money's worth.

So what actually happens if you do fall base over apex and modify your frame in some way?

If you're on one of the main pistes the chances are that help will be on hand within minutes, as the radio-linked ski patrols are on the lookout for unintentional acrobatics. You should stick your skis cross-wise in the snow just uphill of where you're lying, as a sign that you need assistance and to discourage people from ploughing into you. (Avoid doing this if you've just stopped for lunch or your popularity rating will plummet.)

In a more out-of-the-way corner it may be necessary to get an able-bodied skier to go down to the bottom of the tow, where the tow-operator will radio for help.

ACCIDENTS

In an ideal world everyone, especially those who drive cars or indulge in sport, would not only have attended first aid classes but would also have updated their knowledge periodically. All over the country hundreds of people have died from something as simple to remedy as a blocked airway, which need not have been fatal if the first person to come on the scene had known what to do. (Do you?)

Even in downhill skiing, truly life-threatening situations don't crop up as often as one's mother imagines, but the potential is always there. And if you set off into the hills on a ski tour, you immediately assume the responsibility for your own safe return and that of others in your party.

When an accident does occur, its very sudden-ness often has a numbing effect, both on the victim and his/her companions. Yet prompt action can be essential to prevent a fatality, so rather than assume it could never happen to you, it helps to have thought in advance what you would do in the event of, say, an avalanche or someone taking a bad fall.

The first priority is to safeguard the rest of the party. If you are some distance from civilisation, a careful assessment of the situation should be made before any action is taken or decisions made to send someone for help.

When confronted with an inert body it can be hard not to panic at first but this can be overcome by knowing what to do.

In an accident situation, it is often lack of action that kills, rather than someone doing the wrong thing. There is no point in worrying about whether someone has damaged his spine if he is not breathing. Respiratory and cardiac arrest is quite common, especially in avalanche victims, and should be your first concern.

So, how confident are you that you could clear someone's airway, re-establish breathing or carry out chest compression to get the heart beating again? How many compressions to every breath is it? How often should you check the pulse? If you're not one hundred per cent sure, then maybe it's time you took a first aid course. (Addresses of organisations running such courses are listed at the back of this book.)

For more minor on-piste accidents, the walking wounded can seek assistance from the First Aid Posts, known as Wimp Stations on account of their frequent use by those too inefficient to pack a basic first aid kit in the car. It is also the destination of anyone taken off the hill by the rescue team and who requires recuperation facilities, so if someone in your party was last seen heading downhill screaming in terror at 90mph, that is his most likely destination.

CHAPTER SIX

WIDER HORIZONS

THE LURE OF CROSS-COUNTRY SKIING

Some days, when the lift queues stretch endlessly and the nursery slope looks like a vast colony of crippled penguins, even the most ardent downhill freak begins to wonder if this is truly the ultimate experience.

From the top of the highest run a vista of endless shimmering ridges and peaks draws your eye, until it lights on a vast, untouched snowfield glistening in the sun, and suddenly the thought of carving your own tracks over all that deserted virgin snow is totally irresistible.

Or perhaps, after a good snowfall, an anti-cyclone has stationed itself in just the right spot for a run of brilliant days, and the lure of those quiet, crisp forest trails is more than the strongest will can resist.

How, then, do you go about joining the ranks of those oddballs, written off by the average piste-basher as eccentrics, who walk straight up hills on pathetically undernourished skis and vanish down distant corries performing odd little curtseys?

Before you rush off to buy some narrow planks, it's worth considering the different types of cross-country skiing and debating which one is for you.

THE RIGHT EQUIPMENT

A few years ago it was possible to draw a hard and fast line between traditional Nordic skiing, using lightweight skis attached to the boot or shoe at the toe only, and Alpine ski mountaineering, which employed much shorter, broader skis, climbing skins, higher boots and bindings capable of being clipped down at the heel for difficult descents.

Both types of equipment still have their schools of ardent devotees, but because of new ski technology there is now a blurring of the distinctions between them, and the consequent debate about what to go for has become quite complicated. The advent of metal-edged Nordic skis together with new types of boots and bindings has considerably widened the field. With more ankle support and edges that cope with more difficult surfaces, a wider range of turning techniques opens up, and it is now even possible to obtain a Nordic ski with an Alpine flex which gives better turning properties on difficult descents, although it forfeits the traditional Nordic advantage of being able to rely on wax rather than skins for climbing steeper slopes.

A result of these advances is that many more cross-country tourers are taking to the hills on Nordic equipment, tackling slopes and snow conditions hitherto thought fit only for Alpine-type mountain skis. Yet the opinion is still widely held that ski mountaineering in a country known for difficult snow conditions and sudden weather changes calls for the use of Alpine equipment, and it is certain that the great 'skinnies versus fatboards' debate will continue to accompany pints of ale for many years to come.

As the distinctions between the two sports blur, so the manufacturers attempt to fill the gap with more versatile equipment, and especially for the beginner the choice becomes baffling. The best advice is undoubtedly to try out the sport at one of the Nordic ski centres, hiring your equipment until you decide whether you want to buy your own. By then you will have gained the necessary experience to decide just what is for you, and established contacts who will be able to advise you.

The decision as to which type of skis and bindings to go for depends on a number of factors, including the skier's build, strength and experience, but the most important one is defining just what you want to be able to do with your skis.

If the idea of speeding along prepared tracks appeals to you, (reputedly the most aerobically efficient form of exercise known to man), then you will be looking at lightweight Nordic skis, with bindings attaching a special low-cut shoe or boot at the toe only. These skis are built for undulating rather than mountainous terrain, and are used principally on specially-cut tracks and ski trails. Several areas of prepared tracks now exist in Scotland, along with waymarked trails (listed at the end of this chapter) and more will probably follow.

A major advantage of trail skiing over general touring is that it can be enjoyed whatever the weather. The majority of the marked trails are through forestry, and so are sheltered from the wind, one of the factors which has made the sport especially popular with families. There is also an artificial training area at Glenisla.

Once the snow is established on the forest trails, the shade factor means it can be maintained for considerable periods. In the NE Central Highlands, i.e. the area bounded by Speyside, Deeside, Huntly and Inverness, the skiable snow lie is estimated to average 35 days per season.

At Glenisla, Glenmore, Glenmulliach and Inshriach, marked trails have been established through country which lends itself perfectly to cross-country skiing. Maps and, where relevant, trail passes can be obtained from the addresses listed below, and the tours available range from 2 — 3 hours to a full day or even longer if accommodation is organised. They offer a whole new range of experiences, from the sometimes icy thrills of the Canadian trail (Glenmore) and the fine scenery of Glenmulliach, to features like

Body Swerve Bridge and Sharp Intake of Breath Corner in Glenisla.

Anyone wanting to try the sport for the first time will find excellent equipment for hire at or near all the main centres, and many sports shops in towns and cities have now added Nordic skis to their hire range.

It should be remembered that Nordic equipment is not quite as robust as downhill, and needs to be treated with respect, whether hired or bought. A common problem with the three-pin Nordic Norm type binding is failure to fit all three pins into the corresponding holes correctly, often because a walk across the car park has allowed grit to lodge inside them. Many experienced skiers carry a golf tee or some similar little weapon to clean them out, which makes for safer skiing and also extends the life of the equipment.

A full and interesting programme of Nordic events takes place throughout Britain every year, and anyone interested in any aspect — racing, roller skiing, clubs, courses, etc. — should get a copy of the fact-packed Nordic Year Book from Highland Guides, Inverdruie, by Aviemore. (Phone 0479 810 729 for current price).

Parallel Nordic skiing and telemarking are now enjoying a revival on the pistes. Well-executed, the telemark turn is a delight to watch, a graceful ski-curtsey which is beginning to win over downhillers looking for something different. Many Nordic ski schools now offer on-piste tuition in both techniques, making use of the lifts to shorten the learning time.

CROSS-COUNTRY SKI TRAILS

CLASHINDARROCH FOREST, HUNTLY, ABERDEEN-SHIRE
For Trails Map and information Tel. 0466 4161
Five waymarked trails at Clashindarroch East. Car parking.

GLENISLA FOREST, ALYTH, PERTHSHIRE

For Trail Maps and information Tel. 057 582 238
40km of waymarked ski trails and prepared tracks. Artificial track. Ski hire and tuition from Highland Adventure, Knockshannoch Lodge, Glenisla, by Alyth, Perthshire PH11 8PE. Tel. 057 582 238 and 057 582 207.

GLENMORE AND INSHRIACH FORESTS, NR AVIEMORE

For details Tel. 0479 810 729
40km of waymarked trails. Prepared tracks in Glenmore. Ski hire and tuition from Highland Guides, Inverdruie, Aviemore. Tel. 0479 810729.

GLENMULLIE FOREST, NR TOMINTOUL, BANFFSHIRE

For information on packages Tel. 080 74 356
25km of waymarked trails and prepared tracks. Trail Pass, map, car parking, ski shop, restaurant, ski hire and tuition from Glenmulliach Nordic Ski Centre, Tomintoul, Ballindalloch, Banffshire AB3 9ES. Tel. 080 74 356.

CROSS-COUNTRY SKI HIRE

Cairdsport, Aviemore Centre, Inverness-shire. Tel. 0479 810310
Excel Sports, Blairgowrie, Perthshire. Tel. 0250 3859
Glenmulliach Nordic Ski Centre, Tomintoul, Banffshire. Tel. 08074 356
Goodbrand Ski Hire, Corgarff, Strathdon, Aberdeenshire. Tel. 09754 233
Highland Adventure, Knockshannoch, Glenisla, Perthshire. Tel. 05782 238
Highland Guides, Inverdruie, Aviemore, Inverness-shire. Tel. 0479 810729
Mountain Cycles, 9 Harbour Road, Inverness. Tel. 0463 222522

Nevisport, High Street, Fort William. Tel. 0397 4921
Scottish-Norwegian Ski School, Aviemore. Tel. 0479 810656
Sports Hire, Nethybridge, Inverness-shire. Tel. 0479 82353
The Shop, Glenmore, Aviemore, Inverness-shire. Tel. 0479 86253

NORDIC INSTRUCTION/ACCOMMODATION/ HIRE PACKAGES

Glenfeshie Hostel, Glenfeshie, Kincraig, Inverness-shire.
Tel. 05404 323
Basic 5-day touring courses.
Glenmulliach Nordic Ski Centre, Tomintoul, Banffshire. Tel. 08074 356
Basic instruction weekends.
Glenmore Lodge, Aviemore, Inverness-shire PH22 1QU. Tel. 0479 86276
Basic, intermediate & advanced courses.   Telemark workshops.
Highland Activity Holidays, 25 Hillside Ave, Dufftown, Keith, AB5 4AG.
Tel. 0340 20892
Basic & intermediate week/weekend courses.
Highland Adventure, Knockshannoch, Glenisla, Alyth, Perthshire PH11 8PE
Basic, intermediate, advanced. Racing, telemarking. Tel. 0575 82238
Highland Guides, Inverdruie, Aviemore, Inverness-shire PH22 1QH
Variety of basic, intermediate & advanced courses of varying lengths, plus telemarking & mountain skiing.   Tel. 0479 810729
Insh Hall Ski Lodge, Kincraig, Inverness PH21 1NU
2, 5 and 7-day courses, inclusive or self-catering.   Also Ballindalloch Hostel, self-catering only.   Tel. 05404 272

Loch Morlich Youth Hostel, Glenmore, Aviemore, Inverness-shire.
6-day, mainly basic, courses.   Tel. 0479 86 238
Ski Backcountry, Maelstrom, Insh, Kingussie, Inverness-shire PH22 1NT
Intermediate & advanced.   Tel. 054 02 805
Ancrum Outdoor Education Centre, 10 Ancrum Road, Dundee DD2 2H2
Basic & intermediate weekend/day courses.   Tel. 0382 60719

GENERAL TOURING

There is a great deal of scope in Scotland for general ski touring, both low and high level depending on the snow lie.   Metal edged Nordic skis have become very popular both with former hillwalkers who value the increase in range conferred by a pair of skis, and with those who want to branch out from trail skiing or escape from downhill.

There is little point in a discussion of equipment here, since by this stage the skier will have his or her own definite ideas on the subject.   It should be remembered, however, that anyone setting off into the hills should be conversant with the Scottish Mountain Code (outlined below) and always be fully equipped and prepared for sudden changes in the weather.   The ability to use a map and compass is essential, even for low-level routes.

THE ALPINE OPTION

Ski mountaineering, which demands the most robust equipment of all, brings together the skills of both skier and mountaineer.

In its extreme form it can be one of the toughest and most demanding ways of exploring the mountain environment, but even for those whose appetites do not extend to packing their skis up sheer ice faces in order to reach the ultimate ski run, there is plenty of scope to open up new vistas.

Although there is a growing band of extremely skilled ski mountaineers who use Nordic equipment for even the most extreme situations, most ski mountaineering done in Scotland is still on Alpine type equipment. Specialist ski mountaineering skis are somewhat shorter and broader than standard downhill skis, giving them stability in poor snow conditions. They are lighter, which makes them more mobile and easier to carry, and are combined with bindings with full heel lift and safety features. Self-adhesive skins are used for climbing, and boots are taller and stiffer than those used with Nordic skis, but lighter than the downhill version, with adjustment for climbing. Telescopic poles are pleasantly versatile, and ski crampons, ice axe and boot crampons complete the list of essential hardware.

A possible compromise favoured by some is to fit a good and not-too-long pair of downhill skis with a dual-purpose binding, e.g. the Emery Altitude Plus LX Automatic, plus a set of skins. Not all downhill skis would be suitable for this, so advice should be sought, but the system has obvious advantages for downhillers who want to hedge their bets about the weather, crowds etc. One disadvantage is that this binding must be used with safety straps, which can be a hassle if you do a lot of piste skiing and have been thoroughly spoilt by the ease of ski brakes. It does offer possibilities, however, for anyone who wishes to ski the pistes until the crowds build up, then go off touring for the rest of the day.

An important consideration here, however, is that not all downhill skiers have the necessary experience to launch themselves safely into the wilderness. Ski mountaineering is definitely not a discipline to be tackled by the non-mountaineer, since navigation, avalanche and survival skills are vital. Survival gear, first aid kit and emergency rations should always be carried, and a route card left behind 'just in case'.

The best way to get started from scratch is to go on a course. Glenmore Lodge, near Aviemore and Plas-y-Brenin, in North Wales, have interesting ones on offer, or contact the Scottish

Sports Council. Ski clubs are excellent for meeting fellow enthusiasts, and the Scottish Ski Club has an active touring section which holds regular weekend meets throughout the winter.

Recommended guide books include *Ski Tours over Scottish Hills* by Raymond Simpson, *Scottish Mountains on Ski* by Malcolm Slesser and *Ski Mountaineering in Scotland*, edited by Bennet and Wallace and published by the Scottish Mountaineering Trust. Anyone seriously considering taking up ski-mountaineering should also read the superbly illustrated *Skiing Real Snow* by Martin Hurn (Crowood Press) and *Ski Mountaineering* by Peter Cliff (Unwin Hyman). (See book list).

THE SCOTTISH MOUNTAIN CODE

BEFORE YOU GO
Plan within the capabilities of your group.
Ensure you possess the essential equipment.
Refer to the relevant guide books.
Learn the use of map and compass.
Know the weather signs and local forecast.
Know simple first aid and the symptoms of exposure.
Know the mountain distress signals.
Know the country code.
Contact local landowners during stalking and other critical seasons.

WHEN YOU GO
1. Don't go alone until you've gained sufficient experience.
2. Leave written word of your intended route and report back on return.
3. Wear proper footwear (with gaiters in winter).
4. Take warm, windproof and waterproof clothing.
5. Take up-to-date map, compass, whistle, torch, spare food and a survival bag.
6. Avoid disturbance to farming and other land management activities.
7. Be prepared to retreat if weather conditions deteriorate.
8. Remember that descending at the end of the day is the most hazardous time.

CHAPTER SEVEN

'THE ADVANCEMENT OF THE ART'

ADVANCED INSTRUCTION

One of the great things about skiing is that however well you think you ski, there is still more to learn. Those who want to learn more advanced techniques will find that most ski schools can provide a suitable instructor, and it is often worth paying the extra for individual tuition if you want to advance quickly. At Glenshee a new venture called Ski Clinix has been set up, in association with the Cairnwell Ski School, by former British Olympic skiers Clare Booth and Nigel Smith, providing instruction (including the use of video tapes) individually tailored to help people improve their technique. At the Lecht, John Clark, an ex-British Team Coach, runs the ski school and provides training in competitive techniques, including special courses for children and the opportunity to compete in races. Both The Lecht and Glenshee have token-operated race-courses which can be used by the public (see the area guides.)

If you fancy the idea of becoming a ski instructor or taking a ski party leader qualification, contact the British Association of Ski Instructors (BASI), Grampian Road, Aviemore, Inverness-shire, Tel. 0479 810407, for details of courses.

THE RACING SCENE

The Scottish Alpine Race Calendar is now an impressively long document. The Scottish National Ski Council (SNSC) is the main organising body, and the number of racing fixtures grows year by year.

The following explanation of Scottish race training was kindly provided by John Arnold, Director of Coaching for the SNSC.

TRAINING OPPORTUNITIES FOR SCOTTISH SKI RACERS

'Recently within Scotland there have come to exist structured opportunities for ski racers to develop their ability to perform in the Alpine disciplines, Slalom, Giant Slalom and Super Giant Slalom. Downhill skiing does not take place except in the form of Speed Skiing events.

'The training structure may be perceived as an inverted cone, the wide base of the cone representing the great number of participants within ski clubs who form the "grass roots" of the sport. Developing from this core of participants are those whose ability level increases, and as this takes place the number of participants gradually decreases.

......the number of participants gradually decreases.

One reason for this is that each individual's rate of learning and progress varies, and those that are not achieving may cease to participate. Additionally, the more proficient one becomes at a sport, so does the time taken for further improvement become greater. Therefore the narrower end of the cone represents the number of high level performers.

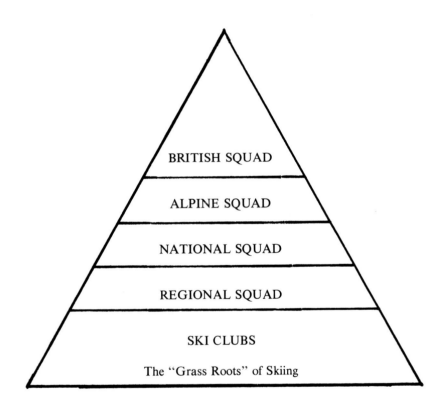

'The training for racing takes place at all levels of ability and is primarily centred around the ski clubs within Scotland. So to get started at ski racing, the first thing to do is to join a ski club that offers a training programme.

'A good training programme should firstly offer training at all levels by qualified and recognised (by the Governing Body, SNSC), skiing coaches. Secondly, the club training should have provision for on-snow and artificial ski slope training on a yearly basis. Thirdly, it should offer physical fitness training (i.e. dry land training) when on-snow training is not possible (eg poor mountain weather conditions). The ski club should also be aware of the dangers of skiing and training, and reflect this awareness in its activities. Established ski clubs also offer social events for the parents, and club buildings on and off the slope.

'A performer can benefit from ski club training throughout the duration of his/her competing career. (Even top class world ski racers like Lesley Beck maintain a close relationship with their 'home' club). If the ski club can provide training for its high level competitors then this is desirable. However, not all ski clubs can sustain this level of training because, for example, they may not have the necessary qualified and experienced staff available, or the financial burden may be too great for the ski club. Therefore, at certain levels of performance the skier may require further training outside the ski club environment.

'It is at this level that the Governing Body, i.e. the Scottish National Ski Council, provides training for high level performers. The SNSC employs experienced, qualified ski coaches who coach performers to varying levels, and at the same time endeavours to assist the member ski clubs in providing training for their performers.

'The SNSC does this in a number of ways, including financial assistance and creating opportunities for ski club coaches to become more knowledgeable.

'One further aspect of the Governing Body's assistance in providing training for racers is the process of recognising and rewarding the performer's ability level. It does this by identifying three levels of performance which are termed Regional, National and Alpine Squads. The individuals who attain the required performance levels are then recognised and rewarded in various ways which include:

* The status of one of the three Squads. (Very useful to help gain sponsorship).
* A skiing uniform and further offers of clothing and equipment either free or at discounted prices.
* Specific Squad training sessions throughout the whole year.
* Assistance to the Squad members' coaches from the ski club in planning and programming the performer's training and competition.
* Financial assistance in the form of grants, and the creating of more opportunities for financial assistance.

'The SNSC adopts a supportive, developmental role within the training structure, with the aim of strengthening the "grass roots" of skiing, so begin the right way and join a ski club.'

The SNSC Coaching Committee co-ordinates a programme in which the major member clubs conduct regular combined training sessions, grooming the young skiers of tomorrow from the 'duckling' stage onwards. Training takes place every weekend throughout the season and continues during the summer on artificial slopes. At Cairngorm, the M1 run is used extensively for racing, and two special courses approved for national racing have recently been laid out at Glenshee, now a World Cup Speed Skiing venue. The Harrier run now provides the Lecht with its own racecourse, and is set to give yet more young racers a start on the ladder.

Fixtures on the Scottish Race Calendar include various British Championships; the North, West and East of Scotland Championships for seniors, children and bairns; schools, army and universities events; the Scottish Mogul Competition and a number of other important races which have attracted some impressively large sponsors.

An up-to-date list of SNSC-affiliated ski clubs is available from: The Scottish National Ski Council, Caledonia House, South Gyle, Edinburgh EH12 9DQ   Tel. 031 317 7280.

THE SKI CLUBS

Ski clubs exist throughout Britain, and encompass many types of activity.

Some are set up mainly as social clubs, holding film and video evenings, primarily as an excuse for a good bevvy. Others take the practical side of skiing very seriously, and run buses to the nearest skiable snow at weekends, often setting up portable lifts of their own. Nordic skiing, touring, ski mountaineering and downhill are all catered for, and can often be tracked down via your nearest dry slope or, in the case of Nordic skiing, with the help of Highland Guides at Inverdruie, whose Year Book yields a fund of vital information. Other sources are The Ski Club of Great Britain and the Scottish Ski Club. (See 'Useful Addresses'). The Scottish Ski Club divides itself into regional sections and has its own huts at Glencoe, Cairngorm and Glenshee. It is closely involved with the race training programme, has a touring section, and its area sections organise a host of other events — film shows, lectures, ski auctions etc.

For children especially, ski clubs often provide the way to greater things. Practically all our racers worked their way up from club races, and even adults who thought they were long past it discover that being in a club improves their skiing enormously. Other attractions include subsidised skiing, cheaper instruction, equipment advice, expeditions, summer activities and special skiing holidays, so it is both surprising and a pity that only an estimated 10% of the skiing British public belong to ski clubs; more widespread involvement at club level could only enhance Britain's prospects of producing winning racers in the future.

The Disabled Ski Club and the Uphill Ski Club are both active in Scotland - see addresses section.

EXTREME SKIING

From the pistes it is sometimes possible to trace the distant trails of the steep-artists, those serpentine flourishes written with an unmistakeably expert hand down the most impossible-looking headwalls. Exclusively the province of the advanced skier whose technical skills and nerve are beyond question, extreme skiing will always appeal to those who enjoy pushing themselves to the limit. For an insight into skiing the steeps and a fascinating list of slopes and angles, the short but informative section by Martin Burrows-Smith in Bennet and Wallace (See above) is well worth reading, along with the listed works on avalanches.

HANG-GLIDING AND PARASCENDING

At Glenshee, Gustav Fischnaller founded the Cairnwell Hang-gliding School in 1974, and has since trained many newcomers in the art. The Cairnwell itself, plus various crags and peaks in the surrounding area, provides literally the jumping-off point for both solo and double flights, and Glenshee has provided the venue for some first-rate competitions and championships.

Like hang-gliding, parascending has also to wait for the right winds and weather for an escape into an entirely new and thrilling world, but has the advantage that less time is taken over rigging: the canopy can be transported up the mountain in a rucksack and takes very little time to spread out ready for take-off. At Glenshee tuition in both sports is available from the Cairnwell Ski School, Tel. 03383 331.

SNOWBOARDING

Halfpipes, cutbacks and lip-launches are all expressions we're likely to hear more of on the Scottish slopes in the next few years, as Scottish skiers start 'breaking free' and getting into the latest trans-Atlantic action.

A major feature on the USA ski scene, snowboarding has had a small but faithful following over here for some time, but now a Scottish Association of Snowboarding has been formed to promote and co-ordinate the sport. The skills required are more allied to surfing and skateboarding than to skiing, and take some time for the newcomer to master — longer than learning to monoski, for instance. Once conquered, however, the results soon become dramatic and the real hotbloods can be seen performing aerial loops, handplants and the like in the halfpipe, a cylindrical track scooped in the snow.

It remains to be seen how resorts over here will react to an escalation in snowboarding; there have been a few areas of conflict abroad, but many Alpine areas are now gearing themselves up to cope with the demand, and more and more competitions and camps are being held in Europe. It is hoped that a snowboarding camp might become a feature on the Scottish calendar: for further details of this and all other aspects of snowboarding contact:

Stuart Duncan, The Scottish Association of Snowboarding, c/o Marywell Gas Supplies, Stonehaven Road, Aberdeen. Tel. 0224 780209 or 867528.

........species you could hope to find......

CHAPTER EIGHT

THE HILLS ARE FOREVER
-OR ARE THEY?

Most skiers probably never think about what lies under the snow. It is quite easy to imagine that the hills are just barren, rock-strewn slopes where next-to-nothing grows, and that the only wildlife you're likely to come across is a party from Leeds having a snowball fight.

Yet the I-Spy spotter's list of the species you could hope to find, especially in the Cairngorms, is surprisingly varied. The granite plateaux, morainic deposits and glaciated corries have given rise to a very distinctive landscape, supporting an arctic flora and fauna which is unique in Britain and which it shares with very few other places in the entire world (Baffin Island is one). The very inhospitability of these mountains has protected them through the ages from exploitation by man and they are now considered to be the most important area for arctic-type wildlife in the EEC.

UPLAND WILDLIFE

So just what might the ardent amateur naturalist hope to see here in the course of a year?

At the higher levels, in addition to the expected heaths and lichens, there is a perhaps surprising range of typical plant, bird and animal species of which the following are examples:

ptarmigan, mountain hare, dotterel, red deer, snow bunting, meadow pipit, crowberry, wheatear, whortleberry, red grouse, stiff sedge, dunlin, wavy hair grass, golden plover, blaeberry, ring ousel, three-leaved rush, peregrine falcon, dwarf juniper, golden eagle.

There are also many species of insects, including moths, found well up the mountainsides, while at lower levels the remnants of the 8,000 year-old Old Caledonian Pine Forest and its many lochans provides habitat for capercaillie, red squirrels. pine martens, wildcats, the Scottish crossbill, crested tits, goldeneye and ospreys. Quite a number of interesting sightings can be had just from the ski road between Aviemore and Coire Cas, and if conditions on the hill or lengthening queues drive you away from the slopes, then even in the winter months a foray around the shores of Loch Morlich can reveal goldeneye, tufted ducks and whooper swans, plus foraging flocks of smaller birds like bluetits. Listen also for the churring trill of the crested tit, and above the treeline watch out for the Cairngorm reindeer herd. These were introduced after the second World War as a potential source of meat for the local population, and have bred here very successfully. The herd is currently near the 80-strong maximum imposed by its grazing range.

Another successful species is the pine marten, which ten years ago was almost exclusively found in the north west of Scotland. The planting of new forests has led to an increase in numbers, and it has now spread as far as Speyside.

THE PRESSURE POINTS

All these creatures form links in a delicate and complex chain, i.e. ANIMALS - BIRDS - INSECTS -VEGETATION - SOIL

Unfortunately the parts of this chain most at risk from skiing are the most vital ones — soil and vegetation. A fragile carpet of plants is all that stabilises the soil and stops it from being washed away by the extreme mountain weather conditions. And far from protecting the vegetation beneath, as you might expect, a layer of snow which is subjected to pressure from above becomes compacted and increases soil erosion. Direct damage from skis is another problem, and is most marked during spring, when melting snow leaves pieces of vegetation protruding above the surface, ready to be sliced off.

Other problems include disturbance of the soil by skilift install-ations, access roads and vehicle tracks, and the covering of vegetation with erosion debris. Where this happens, a slow recovery can take place over a period of several years, provided the depth of the debris is not more than about seven centimetres.

The presence of access roads, chairlifts, car parks and cafes brings increased use of hitherto undisturbed uplands by tourists, hillwalkers and cross-country skiers, so conservationists are concerned about the now discernible outward spread of erosion patterns and the increased encroachment of man into the National Nature Reserves. The spread of litter into these wild areas has strengthened their argument; old beer cans and polythene bags now congregate around most hilltop cairns, themselves fashioned by rock artists whose skills might have been better employed on garden walls.

........around most hill-top cairns.

Pressure on the existing facilities is already extreme

Litter around skiing areas has been shown to attract scavenging predators such as crows, foxes and gulls, which will move in on an area permanently if there is food to support them. Their natural population level would not normally pose a threat to any of the species listed above, but it is now thought their increased numbers may be having an adverse effect on the chicks of dotterel and ptarmigan in some areas. The chairlift companies go to great lengths to remove litter from the hill but the sheer quantity of it is horrifying.

Mountaineering bodies and other groups concerned with the use and management of mountainous areas also resent the intrusion and visual impact of downhill skiing because it detracts from the 'wilderness experience'.

THE DEVELOPER'S CASE

On the other side of the coin we have the arguments put forward by the skiing lobby. It is estimated that over 700,000 skier days are spent at Cairngorm, Glencoe, Glenshee and the Lecht annually, and a conservative estimate of the average annual increase in skiing is between 5% and 10%. This growth, in areas where the population was hitherto in decline, has brought about a substantial increase in jobs, not only in the skiing industry itself but across the board, as small communities have been revived. In Highland Region the population has grown by over 7000 in the last decade, and this growth is expected to continue. The depopulation process in these areas of the Highlands has been reversed, and young people are now able to find jobs near to home instead of having to take off to the cities.

Anyone who has skied during the peak periods will testify that the pressure on the existing facilities is already extreme, with queue lengths in some places becoming ridiculous. This gives rise to another point to ponder: if downhill skiers become disenchanted by the length of lift queues, will substantial numbers take to cross-country skiing instead? There is already a natural progression to the ski trails of downhillers who have had enough of crowds, while those who have cut their XC teeth on the trails are now heading upwards to the more remote mountainous areas in search of new experiences. If there was to be a significant increase in this form of recreation, the long-term effect on a much larger area could be serious.

It is also argued that the total area affected by skiing developments is very small in relation to the vastness of the Scottish Highlands, and that the areas already under conservation designation are sufficiently large to protect the future of the upland environment.

There is, of course, no easy solution to the controversy. Campaigns with emotive titles are snapped up by the media and serve to fuel the popular image of the conservationists as over-protective, fanatical 'greenies' and the ski developers as ruthless, get-rich-quick landgrabbers.

Yet both sides have perfectly valid arguments. There is a need for more skiing development, and it would undoubtedly benefit the Scottish economy. There is also the ever-present danger that what man has already done to vast areas of the globe — the Great Dustbowl, the tropical rain forest, the mountains of Nepal — will ultimately happen here, in the interests of commercial gain. Once these areas have been destroyed, they have gone for ever.

PRACTICAL STEPS FORWARD

What, then, is being done to try and resolve the conflicts of interest? Moves have, in fact, been in play for several years but they seldom get into the newspapers. In 1984 the Scottish Development Department published the National Planning Guidelines on skiing developments in Scotland. Its aim was to reconcile development needs with conservation interests and the analysis of potential areas for skiing expansion was based on the Langmuir survey of 1979, when a group of expert skiers tested out all the areas considered to have potential and reported on their findings.

The Nature Conservancy Council provided an inventory of the nature conservation interests in each area, and the probable impact of skiing development, and Highland Regional Council's Winter Sports Working Party studied skiing demand and the viability of the various areas.

As a result of this, guidelines for both primary and secondary ski areas were drawn up, together with a framework for assessing development plans and proposals. (Copies of the guidelines, for anyone interested, can be obtained from the Scottish Development Department, Planning Services, Room 5/93, New St Andrew's House, Edinburgh EH1 3SZ.)

At a practical level, in June 1986 ASH Environmental Design produced an exceedingly detailed tome entitled *'Environmental Design and Management of Ski Areas in Scotland — A Practical Handbook*, for the Countryside Commission for Scotland and Highland Regional Council. Its main function was to provide a planning framework for ski developments, and it was compiled in consultation with a number of bodies, including the Nature Conservancy Council, the chairlift companies, national sports bodies and the Highlands and Islands Development Board.

The result is a very practical volume, filled with diagrams and a wealth of information on planning and design, plus the materials and techniques which will help to minimise the adverse effects of ski developments on the environment. Aspects such as erosion, hydrology, wildlife disturbance, visual impact, pollution and visitor management are all dealt with, and there has been ongoing communication and co-operation between all the bodies concerned. Assessments are made at the beginning and end of every season and the level of awareness of environmental considerations is very high. Summer visitors to Cairngorm, for instance, will be able to see the large areas which have been re-seeded, plus the extensive drainage system which normally lies hidden under the snow. Such features may not look terribly natural but they are a vital form of insurance for the hill's future.

SAFEGUARDING OUR OWN FUTURE

The destiny of the Scottish hills does not, however, lie purely in the hands of large organisations. The individual skier, whether downhill or cross-country, can do several things to help safeguard the fragile uplands which support his sport. The idea of the odd discarded chocolate wrapper harming the future of the ski industry sounds ludicrous, yet when you consider that 10,000 skiers may be using a resort in one day, the extent of the litter problem becomes more real. The time spent by employees picking up litter, both on the slopes and in the cafes, has to be paid for in the ticket price. In some resorts in the the USA, skiers 'buzz' their own tables after meals, and are rewarded by cheaper day tickets.

Even bio-degradable litter such as bread crusts, banana skins and apple cores can cause problems, because it encourages scavengers like carrion crows and foxes, which in turn inflict casualties on chicks in the spring.

Time spent picking up litter

Spring, of course, is the vulnerable time, when patches of bare ground and vegetation begin to show, and the damage done to emerging plants can be very high. It takes the passage of relatively few pairs of skis to scythe off heather and other species, and once the gaps appear the soil will begin to wash away. It is a slow, insidious, ongoing process which the individual will never notice, but the cumulative effects of constant passage are considerable. So wherever possible, avoid skiing over bare patches.

Where a ski area is bounded by a National Nature Reserve or a Site of Special Scientific Interest, it is important to respect the markers and stay within them. A set of tracks setting off into the unknown only encourages others to follow. The areas immediately beyond the tops of lifts would rapidly become degraded were it not for the resrictions, which is why those who ignore the notices risk having their ticket confiscated.

The cross country skier has a greater responsibility to the environment, since he or she is venturing into the fragile areas which will show the ill effects of human impact most rapidly. Not dropping litter and avoiding direct damage to the vegetation are obvious guidelines, but less so is the need to avoid snow compaction. If a group of skiers crosses a snow field in single file, each following in the tracks of the leader, there will be a considerably greater impact on the ground and vegetation beneath than if they spread out, each making their own way. It takes very little time for discernible tracks to appear over such areas, and one single track is more likely to be followed by subsequent skiers.

Another point of which skiers may be less aware is the danger of moving red deer off their wintering grounds. Wintertime for them means a hard struggle for survival and the few hours in a day which a herd spends foraging on an area of more productive ground can be vital. Repeated disturbance by skiers or walkers can severely restrict their grazing range. Grouse and ptarmigan are also adversely affected by repeated intrusion into areas where they congregate in winter.

Early morning sensations

An interest in upland wildlife can considerably enhance the skier's enjoyment of wilderness areas, and hopefully those who are aware of the potential problems will be willing to make the occasional detour and will ensure that all their litter goes home with them. Who knows, they may even start adding binoculars to their list of essential equipment?

KNOWING THE ISSUES

The most vital contribution that every skier can make, however, is to become acquainted with the facts, both of upland conservation and of the development needs of the ski industry. Many of the fiery arguments which take place in pubs are based on little or no knowledge of the real issues or their background, whereas taking the trouble to find out could replace a lot of the hot air with the kind of informed reasoning the whole debate deserves.

Scottish skiing derives its unparalleled appeal from a unique blend of mountain scenery and climate, plus the character and hardiness of its participants. The early-morning sensations of slanting golden sunlight, the icy air hitting your lungs, the tantalising expanse of new snow stretched before your ski tips....it seems as if time stands still in that magical instant before you push off, wondering what new experiences today will bring.

One thing is for certain; it won't be like yesterday!

THE SCOTTISH DOWNHILL SKI CENTRES

Getting to know a ski area takes time. Most skiers recall the traumas they underwent when they tackled a demon draglift for the first time, or took a wrong turn onto the blue run and ended up stuck in the snowfence. And experienced skiers, too, can waste a lot of time finding out that the run they've just spent half an hour queuing for takes them four minutes to get down and was no great thrill either.

When the time you have available for skiing is short, you want to make the most of it. Each of the following descriptions has been supplied by someone who has skied that particular area for years and knows it really well, so hopefully it will provide something of a shortcut to more and better skiing.

GAELIC PLACE NAMES

For those who do not have the Gaelic, some of the names mentioned may seem well nigh unpronounceable, so here is a list of some of the main ones, together with a brief definition. Sometimes there is more than one possible definition. Not all the names are necessarily pronounced correctly on the ski grounds: e.g. Carn Aosda is more commonly pronounced *kaarn osda* than the correct *kaarn oesh*, but if you get the odd funny look you can at least console yourself that you may be incomprehensible, but you are correct.

The stressed syllable or word in Gaelic is usually the second, the normal position of the adjective or qualifying word.

GLENCOE (Glen Coe) - narrow glen, or glen of the river Coe.

Meall a' Bhuiridh (myowl a vooree) - hill of the bellowing (of the stags).

THE LECHT - stony slope/the declivity.

GLENSHEE (Glen Shee) - glen of the fairy hill.

Cairnwell (usually Cairn Well) (from Carn Bhalg, pronounced kaarn valak) - hill of the bags or the bulges hill.

Carn Aosda (kaarn oesh) is the local pronunciation; probably from Carn Aoise, meaning Hill of Age.

Glas Maol (glas moel) - greenish-grey bare hill.

Caenlochan Probably derived from Cadha an lochan (cah'n lochan) - steep place (or pass) of the little loch.

Tom Dearg (towm dyerak) - red hill.

Coire Fionn (kora fyoon) - white corrie.

Meall Odhar (myowl oa'ar) - brown hill.

AVIEMORE (avie more) - the big hill face or the great gap.

Cairngorm (kayrn gorm or gorram) - blue hill.
Coire Cas (kora cass) - steep corrie.
Fiacaill a' Choire Chais (feeachkal a chorra chahish) - tooth of
Coire Cas. Often simply referred to as Fiacaill.
Coire an t-Sneachda (kor an trachka) - corrie of the snow.
Allt Coire an t-Sneachda (owlt kor an trachka) - stream of Coire an
t-Sneachda.
Coire na Ciste (kora na kistya) - corrie of the chest/coffin.
An t-Aonach (an toenach) - the hill or the height.
Dalwhinnie (from dail chuinnidh) - the champions' field.
Aonach Mor (an ach more) - the great hill.

CAIRNGORM

The ski slopes at Cairngorm are just a few miles from Aviemore, reached by a scenic access road which passes through sections of the Old Caledonian pine forest. Since the chairlift was first opened in December 1961, the expansion of the ski slopes has led to corresponding developments in accommodation and leisure pursuits in the Spey Valley, which is now a thriving tourist area.

When you reach the upper section of the access road you will be faced with the day's first decision: which car park to choose...left to Coire na Ciste or right to Coire Cas? At the height of the season you may have no choice, as the main car park at Coire Cas fills early, but if you are a beginner or inexperienced skier this is the one to aim for. All the most suitable runs are here, and it is also where the ski schools meet, most beside the Day Lodge. There is a free bus service between the two car parks, and tickets can be bought on either side. In the main hall of the Day Lodge, where tickets are on sale, there is also a snack bar, a bar, a restaurant, toilets, ski hire and an equipment shop.

From the Coire Cas Car Park there are four routes up the hill. The Car Park Chair is used by beginners, and can be very busy even early in the day, more so at weekends. On all chairlifts a child must be accompanied by an adult.

The Fiacall Ridge Poma is a fast alternative for intermediates upwards, and takes you above the Fiacall T-Bar, Coire Cas T-Bar, the M1 Poma, the White Lady Chair and the White Lady T-Bar, all of which are reached by turning left and schussing across one or more of the runs. Before traversing, do check by looking above you so that you avoid spoiling someone's descent as you cross. A more direct and steeper line towards the Day Lodge takes you onto

CAIRNGORM RUNS

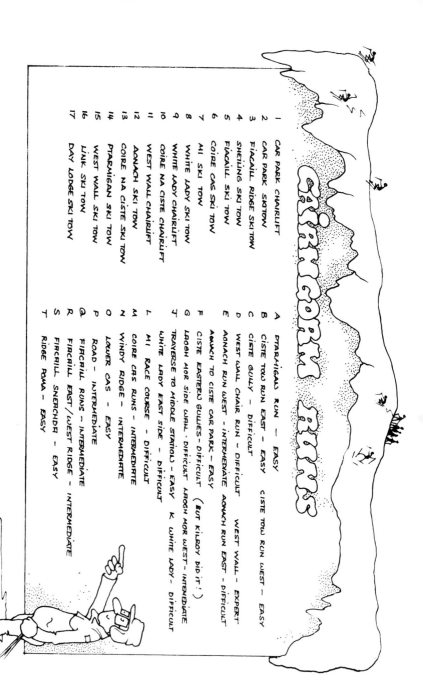

1. CAR PARK CHAIRLIFT
2. CAR PARK SKITOW
3. FIACAILL RIDGE SKI TOW
4. SHEILING SKI TOW
5. FIACAILL SKI TOW
6. COIRE CAS SKI TOW
7. M1 SKI TOW
8. WHITE LADY SKI TOW
9. WHITE LADY CHAIRLIFT
10. COIRE NA CISTE CHAIRLIFT
11. WEST WALL CHAIRLIFT
12. AONACH SKI TOW
13. COIRE NA CISTE SKI TOW
14. PTARMIGAN SKI TOW
15. WEST WALL SKI TOW
16. LINK SKI TOW
17. DAY LODGE SKI TOW

A. PTARMIGAN RUN — EASY
B. CISTE TOW RUN EAST — EASY   CISTE TOW RUN WEST — EASY
C. CISTE GULLY — DIFFICULT
D. WEST WALL CHAIR RUN — DIFFICULT   WEST WALL — EXPERT
E. AONACH RUN WEST — INTERMEDIATE   AONACH RUN EAST - DIFFICULT
F. ABNACH TO CISTE CAR PARK - EASY
G. CISTE EASTERN GULLIES - DIFFICULT   (BUT KILROY DID IT!)
H. LAOGH MOR SIDE WALL - DIFFICULT   LAOGH MOR WEST - INTERMEDIATE
J. TRAVERSE TO MIDDLE STATION - EASY   K. WHITE LADY - DIFFICULT
   WHITE LADY EAST SIDE - DIFFICULT
L. M1 RACE COURSE - DIFFICULT
M. COIRE CAS RUNS - INTERMEDIATE
N. WINDY RIDGE - INTERMEDIATE
O. LOWER CAS - EASY
P. ROAD - INTERMEDIATE
Q. FIRCRILL RUNS - INTERMEDIATE
R. FIRCRILL EAST/WEST RIDGE - INTERMEDIATE
S. FIRCRILL SNEACHDA - EASY
T. RIDGE POMA - EASY

106

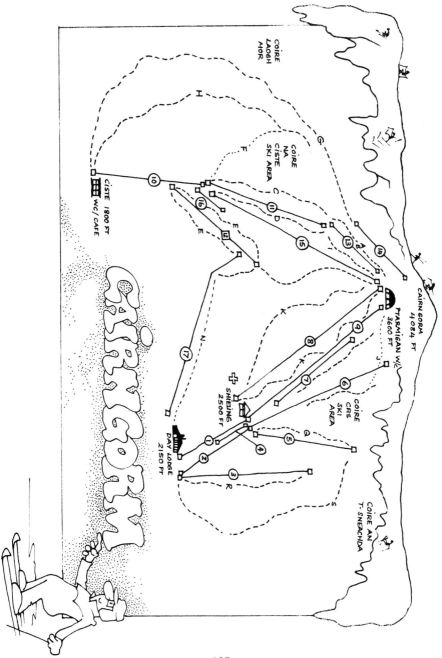

CAIRNGORM

COIRE LAOGH MOR

COIRE NA CISTE SKI AREA

CISTE 1800 FT
WC/CAFE

CAIRN GORM 4084 FT

PTARMIGAN WC 3600 FT

SHIELING 2500 FT

DAY LODGE 2150 FT

COIRE CAS SKI AREA

COIRE AN T-SNEACHDA

a wide unmarked slope frequently used for race training and minor races. It can occasionally hold good powder and can also be reached by turning right off the Fiacall T-Bar and starting down the ridge to the top of the poma. This avoids the less exciting lower slopes and larger queues.

Turning right off the Fiacall Ridge Poma takes you onto a little-used run of fairly even gradient where the turns to the left are longer than those to the right. The snow is frequently soft and unconsolidated, making it a little more difficult than pisted slopes. It is sometimes worth an early morning run but unfortunately it takes you back to an ever-increasing queue.

An alternative access is by the Car Park Tow. Gentle and slow, it has a short downhill section three quarters of the way up which throws the unwary when they overtake the T-Bar reel.

This brings you to just below the Coire Cas T-Bar queue area at what can often be a bottleneck where relieved beginners pause to contemplate their next heart-fluttering experience. Exit to the left along the track towards the Chairlift station and the Shieling.

The run back down leads between the snow fences of the beginners' area where, depending on their positioning, there can be deep gullies at the narrow points with giggling prostrate bodies to be avoided.

Passing the bottom of the Shieling Tow (the gentle beginners' poma) on an all but flat track, remember to mind your head on the upcoming chair if there is deep snow. You have a choice at the end of this track: right takes you down the gully of a stream which, when filled, is a gentle series of swinging turns but when incomplete leaves a steeper left hand bank only. It is not unknown for those with limited control to take an early bath.

Left takes you towards the Car Park Tow and another gentle slope, but in spring this frequently turns to slush and even running water for ten to fifteen yards, with opportunities for learning to water ski. In spite of attempts to organise the waiting for the Car

.........take an early bath!

Park Tow, the queue frequently straggles up the slope in single file for a couple of hundred yards.

New for the 1988 - 89 season was the Day Lodge Poma, which takes you over the ridge to Aonach and gives access to the runs dealt with in that section, plus the newly-fenced area.

If you can avoid having to return to the car park at lunchtime at the height of the season, and particularly at weekends, do so. By staying up the mountain you avoid wasting a lot of time queueing to get back up.

In late spring and sometimes at the beginning of the season it is impossible to ski right back to the Day Lodge, so you will need to use the Chairlift, the downhill entrance being on the opposite side of the building from where you alighted.

Coire Cas is an extremely popular run. It is gentle and forgiving at the top with alternative starts depending on snow conditions. It is normal to leave the tow to the right, but sometimes possible to start the descent from the left, though the direct line can be narrow and overtaking difficult.

The run narrows and steepens at the last quarter at the well-known Gun Barrel. Everybody has their Gun Barrel story. It moguls quickly but gets pisted when things become too hectic and the prone body count reaches critical levels. This is a good run for the competent skier to warm up on but to be avoided if you want a memorable and trouble-free last run, unless of course you're keen on a slalom with erratically-moving human poles.

A potential disaster area is at the top of the Gun Barrel where you should watch for skiers arriving at speed from top right.

If you wish to avoid the Gun Barrel (it may be closed early in the season until it fills), then follow the signs to the left along a series of zig-zag fences to the bottom.

With good snow conditions it is possible to turn off to the left half way down the Gun Barrel, cross the tow track and ski a wider unmogulled slope to the queue.

The Fiacall T-Bar is a good run once you have mastered the beginners' slopes. After a short initial traverse to the left of the tow, there is a fairly wide but even descent to the snow fences leading from the top of the Gun Barrel. If snow permits, a relatively direct route will take you down, but it is generally easier to follow the fences until you have assessed the conditions and possibilities.

From the top of the Fiacall the unpatrolled but fenced slopes of Coire an t Sneachda can be reached by coming off to the right. Here, when it's quiet, you can get an insight into some of the attractions of cross-country skiing. Follow the markers down the glen until you round the hill above the car park.

The M1 run was created for racing and is frequently command-eered for this purpose, especially at weekends. It therefore makes little sense to ski it for fun when the flags are out. The M1 Poma allows racers and trainers with priority bibs the right to feed directly into the head of the queue on a one-for-one basis. You may therefore, on a lousy day, see the same 'wunderkind' go up twice before you reach the exit gate.

111

The M1 is of a moderate though gradually increasing gradient on the first half, becoming wider and gentler lower down before steepening again after the timing hut, just above the queue.

Heading further right off the top of this tow takes you along the Traverse, a schuss to the head of Coire Cas. This is the normal descent for relative beginners who have been skiing the upper gentle slopes of Coire na Ciste. Go into a tuck if there is the slightest headwind as the gradient all but disappears before the sharp bend, from where it's down a short moderate incline onto the narrow road which runs above and parallel to Coire Cas — with a marginally steeper gradient than the piste below.

Left off the M1 Poma takes you onto the White Lady run, a wide moderate slope which moguls with use. At the bottom of this are the Elephant Fences where a high drift offers a relatively safe spot to stop and contemplate the narrower, steep section which produces the biggest and best moguls. To return to the M1 Tow it

........stop and contemplate.

It passes under the chairlift.

is necessary to traverse left well above the bottom of the White Lady, while straight down with a slight relaxation of gradient takes you to the White Lady T-Bar, probably the busiest on the hill. It may on a windy day be the only access for all levels of skier to the gentler slopes of Coire na Ciste, and can prove a difficult tow for the inexperienced.

Having got to the top, there are two ways to approach the White Lady Run proper. The direct route along the tow can be relatively snowless at times but saves pushing into a strong westerly wind and tackling the awkward narrows in the snow fences. The longer but more popular track leads more directly away from the right of the lift. It passes under the Chairlift (reserve your best parallels for those studying critically from above), turns right and narrows into a bottleneck close to where those coming off the M1 also hit the top of the Lady. This section frequently moguls with no room for error, but just let the skis flow and you'll find yourself on the wide upper White Lady.

On rare occasions, snow conditions permitting, it is possible to turn left off the tow, ski the gentle fenced piste to above the Shieling, then drop down a steep, exhilarating slope to just above the Scottish Ski Club Hut. There are quite a number of edge-blunting stones on this route, and unfortunately it rarely lasts.

The area served by the Ptarmigan Tow and the Coire na Ciste Tow consists of a large, gentle bowl which lasts right through to the end of the season. In the middle of winter it can be very exposed, witness the name plate on the Tow hut - 'Ice Station Zebra'.

Short, gentle off-piste runs are to be found by turning left off the Ptarmigan Tow, traversing to various points above the bowl and selecting a suitable route back down to the piste. It is not unknown to get reasonable powder in this area and to be able to leave clearly identifiable tracks.

By continuing further along the ridge, expert skiers can find exciting steep off-piste skiing in Coire Laogh Mor. The steepest (watch you don't bowl over the odd apprentice snow-and-ice

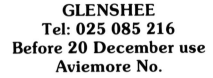

climber) is found by skating and pushing to the right across the very gentle ridge until you reach the headwall. (Know your conditions: it avalanches, as does the head wall of Coire Cas). The views to east and west from here are definitely worth a pause.

A less steep but nonetheless enjoyable descent is gained by dropping off the wide and moderate slope of the East Wall until you find the snow fence leading to your right. Before setting out, make sure the snow fence run from Coire Laogh Mor to the Coire na Ciste car park is complete. This run is sometimes posted closed and should not be attempted if the mist has closed in and you are unfamiliar with the geography of the area.

The remaining steep lower half of the East Wall takes you to the bottom of the gully, opposite the board walk to the West Wall Chair. These boards are needed in late spring for access from the end of the Gully (by then well-mogulled) to the lift, but at the height of the season it is skiable.

The Gully itself is moderately steep but narrow and can catch out intermediates who have found Coire na Ciste easy and the continuation inviting. After it has filled in a strong wind, however, it provides a smooth, fast run with escape routes, should it be necessary, up the side walls. When it moguls, the Gully can become congested with stationary skiers pondering their next move.

Alternative uplift from this point can be had by using the West Wall Poma which terminates beside the top of the White Lady Tow and therefore aids rapid return to the Cas side.

If you wish to ski the West Wall only or the steeper section of The Gully, The West Wall Chair provides access.

The West Wall itself is a broad, steep convex slope which is for better skiers only. It can be closed due to ice and these notices should be heeded, since a fall under these conditions can be fatal. If you are enjoying a direct and ever-steepening descent, watch out for the stepped 'roads' created by those traversing from

Corrour House Hotel

Inverdruie, Aviemore.
Inverness-shire. PH22 1QH.

A lovely country house Hotel, set in four acres of secluded garden and woodland, with marvellous views of the Lairig Ghru Pass and the Cairngorm Mountains.

There are ten spacious bedrooms with private facilities, lounges with cosy log fires and excellent food and wine. A relaxed and homely atmosphere where country lovers are assured of a warm welcome from hosts, David and Sheana Catto.

Ski Packages, ski hire and tuition arranged.
Scottish Tourist Board: Three Crowns Commended.
For Brochure and Tariff, Tel: (0479) 810220.

THE SILVERFJORD HOTEL
Ruthven Road, Kingussie, Inverness-shire.

The village of Kingussie nestles at the foot of Creag Bheag, in the splendour of the Spey valley. It is an ideal centre for touring and hill walking, and for all the other delights of the Highlands.

Here at the Silverfjord, quite simply we serve the best food around. Bar meals and dinners can be complemented from an excellent wine list.

When you stay with us, you will find that the rooms are very comfortable (some with private baths), with wash basins, electric blankets, tea making facilities and central heating.

For a friendly atmosphere with a personal touch under the supervision of Margaret Fraser, telephone:-

(05402) 292   Guests: 342.

the Gully to the West Wall Poma — they can be a severe test to the shock absorbers.

Access to The Wall can be difficult. Turning right off the Chair leads to a snow fence and a short, narrow and frequently rocky descent. Coming left off the Chair usually provides access without dropping all the way into the Gully before finding a traverse to the left. Between the Chair and the Poma the fenced run produces good moguls on a fairly uniform and less steep slope than The Wall itself. The contrast with the relatively un-mogulled other side of the Chair is frequently visible from Glenmore.

Aonach, with its Poma, can be reached by the new access tow from above the Day Lodge and also by a long and in places very gentle descent from the top of Coire na Ciste, via Windy Ridge, where the White Lady Tow meets the West Wall Poma. Unfortunately from this point the size of the queue is unknown, and once you get down there you are committed to wait, unless conditions allow a return to the Ciste car park and a trip back up the Chair, from which the Aonach queue can be seen.

Aonach is a broad bowl with a steep start and a concave fall line. Skiers normally get off to the left of the tow, begin with a traverse and break off when they find a free line. When snow is scarce, the gentle lower slope narrows, but beware the final short descent into the queue, particularly when the tops of the snow fences are sticking through. This tow line is the lowest, so it is usually the last to be complete and the first to break.

From the top of the Aonach, access to the Shieling Area can be gained by following the signs and snow fences to the right. A challenging steep slope to the left can provide an interesting descent in the right conditions.

From the bottom of The Gully or of Aonach it is also possible, on a gentle but tricky schuss, to reach the restaurant at Coire na Ciste Car Park.

LYNWILG HOTEL · AVIEMORE

LOCH ALVIE

Tel. (STD Code 0479) 810207

Relax in the warm and friendly atmosphere of this traditional family-run Hotel overlooking Loch Alvie, set in Kinrara forest, about 1½ miles south of Aviemore Centre.
Comfortable rooms, some with private bath and toilet. In the Stag Restaurant, you will enjoy the best of local produce, beautifully prepared and served.
There is skiing close by, and the Hotel will arrange hire of equipment and instruction. Fishing is available, with 3½ miles of the Spey, as well as other excellent waters. Stalking and rough shooting, golf, climbing, walking, gliding, riding, windsurfing, and canoeing, all available locally.
Or you can just relax in this most glorious part of the Scottish Highlands.
Special weekend and weekday breaks.

AA
★ ★

The GLEN

RAC
★ ★

hotel and restaurant

Newtonmore, Inverness - Shire. PH20 1DD.
Telephone: (05403) 203

Stay with us, and enjoy superb home-cooked meals and the warm, friendly atmosphere of our well-stocked bar in the heart of the Highlands.
OPEN TO NON-RESIDENTS

120

The Coire na Ciste Chair is not for the inexperienced. Unlike the Chairs on the Coire Cas side, the ascent is made with your skis on, and to alight, you ski down a ramp. When the hill is busy and latecoming beginners are forced to use this access, sadistic sports fans can enjoy a comedy of errors as bodies slither and tumble down the ramp.

Downhill passengers are taken on the lower chair, but there is no such facility on the upper, except in an emergency. Beginners using this route for access to the gentle upper slopes frequently have difficulty returning to the car park, and it is not an uncommon sight to see a pathetic figure, hugging skis, plodding laboriously down beside the West Wall. This is a dangerous method of descent if there is any ice around. Instead, head for the Traverse, then down Coire Cas and the Car Park Run to the Day Lodge, from where there is a free bus service back to Coire na Ciste Car Park.

Facilities for eating on the hill are good considering the numbers catered for. The Shieling, Ptarmigan and Coire na Ciste have cafes, and there is space for eating packed lunches under cover. The Scottish Ski Club have a hut just above the Shieling which provides shelter and catering for members and their guests only.

Latest petrol: MacRae & Dick, open 8am - 10pm. They also run a 24hr breakdown recovery service, Tel. 0479 810224, as do Grants of Aviemore, Tel. 0479 810232, and The Old Bridge Garage, Carrbridge, Tel. 0479 84 254 (daytime)/ 0479 84 277 (night).

Enquiries about skiing at Cairngorm to:
The General Manager, Cairngorm Chairlift Company, Aviemore.
Tel. 0479 8626

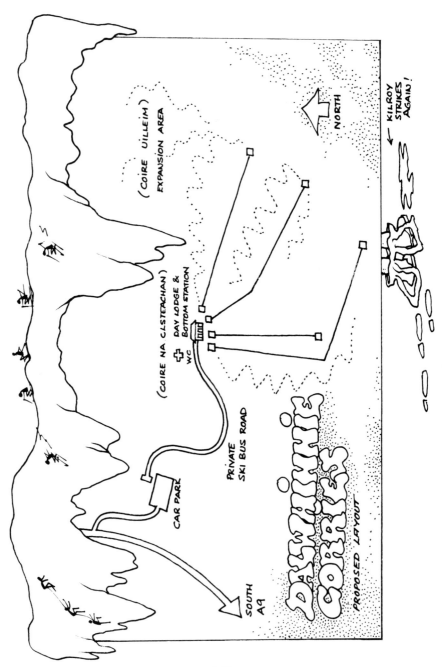

DALWHINNIE CORRIES

PROPOSED LAYOUT

(Coire Uilleim)
EXPANSION AREA

(Coire na Cisteachan)

DAY LODGE &
BOTTOM STATION

WC

PRIVATE
SKI BUS ROAD

CAR PARK

SOUTH
A9

NORTH

← KILROY
STRIKES
AGAIN!

DALWHINNIE CORRIES

Winter travellers of the A9 have long been aware of the snow potential of the Drumochter area, and hopefully will be glad to hear that it is to be put to good use.

One of Scotland's newest ski developments, the Dalwhinnie Corries area will be served by a car park just off the A9, less than one mile from the village of Dalwhinnie (hitherto probably best known for its picturesque distillery). From the car park skiers will be transported by shuttle bus the remaining three quarters of a mile to the restaurant, although skiers arriving by coach will be taken directly to the restaurant and the coach will then return to the car park.

The skiing will take place in Coire nan Cisteachean, where there will be four main tows of approximately 350 metres each in length. There will also be two small beginners' tows close to the restaurant, which will be sited at the 600 metre level, with the tows rising from there to the top of the mountain at 950 metres.

Nearest petrol: Dalwhinnie Garage, 8.30am - 7.30pm weekdays, 8.30am - 1pm Saturday, 10am -7.30pm Sunday. Breakdown service same hours, telephone Dalwhinnie 267.

As further information, particularly about the intended opening date, becomes available, it will be put out on the Ski Hotline - 0898 654 661.

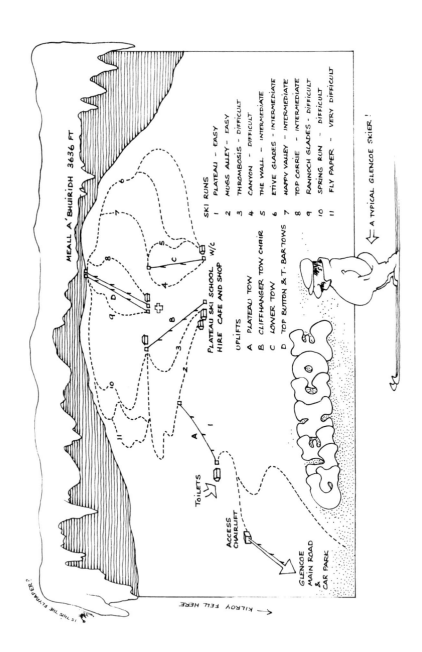

MEALL A'BHUIRIDH 3636 FT

SKI RUNS
1 PLATEAU - EASY
2 MUGS ALLEY - EASY
3 THROMBOSIS - DIFFICULT
4 CANYON - DIFFICULT
5 THE WALL - INTERMEDIATE
6 ETIVE GLADES - INTERMEDIATE
7 HAPPY VALLEY - INTERMEDIATE
8 TOP CORRIE - INTERMEDIATE
9 RANNOCH GLADES - DIFFICULT
10 SPRING RUN - DIFFICULT
11 FLY PAPER - VERY DIFFICULT

⟸ A TYPICAL GLENCOE SKIER !

PLATEAU SKI SCHOOL
HIRE CAFE AND SHOP

UPLIFTS
A PLATEAU TOW
B CLIFFHANGER TOW CHAIR
C LOWER TOW
D TOP BUTTON & T. BAR TOWS

GLENCOE

Toilets

ACCESS
CHAIRLIFT

GLENCOE
MAIN ROAD
&
CAR PARK

IS THIS THE FLYPAPER ?

⟵ KILROY FELL HERE ⟶

124

GLENCOE

THE RUNS

For varied and challenging skiing in a compact area, Glencoe has a lot to offer. It is a small, convivial hill with a long skiing history. In the 1930's the Creag Dhu Mountaineering Club and the Lomonds club used Ba Cottage as a doss and the base for their skiing activities, amid a good-natured rivalry. These two clubs eventually gave birth to the Glencoe Ski Club and the White Corries Rescue Patrol, and before long the Scottish Ski Club joined in the action. Frith Finlayson set up his ski school, and Glencoe became a Mecca for Glasgow-based skiers. Today it still draws many of its devotees from the banks of the Clyde, but improved uplift facilities, particularly the new Plateau Tow, mean that it now caters for a much wider skiing public.

Glencoe is normally open only at weekends, and from February onwards on Fridays and Mondays also. At Easter it is open for the whole holiday period. The skiing area is reached by a single chairlift which formerly deposited one on the edge of the plateau with a bracing walk in prospect before the tows would be reached. Now, however, the poma will take you to within easy reach of the higher lifts. A new addition at Glencoe is a pisteing machine, which should enhance the skiing a lot.

The Plateau. The new tow and fencing on the plateau has opened up some enjoyable new runs for the novice, relieving the congestion of Mugs' Alley, and also providing uplift back up the hill for those good skiers adventurous enough to ski the East Ridge (a steep, exposed, long run usually on virgin snow — the best on the hill).

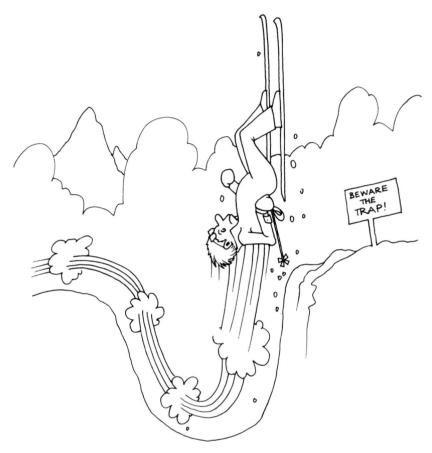

The Haggis Trap.

Mugs' Alley. Starting with the easy runs, Mugs' Alley provides a nice warm-up for the first few runs of the day and, as its name implies, is very popular with the less confident skiers. The gradient on one side is steeper than on the other, so gives a choice of descent, and the run culminates in the canyon under the chairlift. You can distinguish the canyon by the number of hotdogging adolescents flying by. At weekends Mugs' Alley is very crowded and is strictly for the novice.

Etive Fields. On very icy days when the top of the hill may be closed, it is worth the effort, after leaving the bottom T-bar, to walk up maybe 50 yards of hill in order to ski down as far to the left as possible. This provides a nice gentle long run, usually not as icy as the rest of the hill, rejoining the T-bar back at the bottom.

Happy Valley. When the snow is good, Happy Valley is a great fun run, with moguls from top to bottom. If you want to avoid the moguls, however, ski slightly further to the left (west). This run fans out into a number of descents, so you can choose your own way back to the tows. At the bottom of Happy Valley lies 'The Haggis Trap'. Usually the first indication of its presence is the sudden appearance of a hotdogger launching out of a hole in the ground, and should preferably be viewed from downhill to get the full effect of gritted teeth, contorted expressions and crash landings. The Trap itself is best described as a wee gully with vertical entry and exit slopes where you're guaranteed to part company with your stomach.

Rannoch Glades. This is a fairly gentle run between Happy Valley and the Spring Run. It's quite interesting to pick your way through the rocks in search of unskied snow, of which there's usually plenty. You can either cut off near the bottom to rejoin the upper tows, or carry on down a steeper section to rejoin Mugs' Alley. There is also the option of descending Coire Ba, a great run when conditions are right.

The Spring Run. To find the Spring Run you turn left off the top of the tow and traverse east across the top of the hill, where a

127

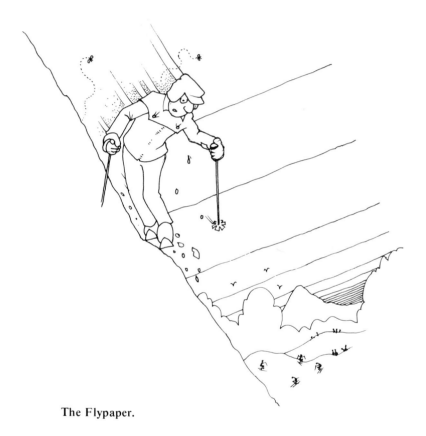

The Flypaper.

track leads through the stones. It's somewhat steeper than Happy Valley with fewer moguls — a good run for those sticky days when the snow is like porridge, since the extra steepness provides more momentum to stop skis from sticking to the snow. Again you have the option of leaving it near the bottom to go back up, or head on down Mugs' Alley. A good route to the snack bar.

Flypaper. This is the steepest marked run on the hill and is very short but quite vicious, with rocks poking out half way down. Fall here in icy conditions and you'll be more than lucky to escape unscathed. Waist deep in powder, however, it's a fabulous run, and like the Canyon and Haggis Trap, is a favourite with the lunatic schoolies.

Another reasonably demanding run is above Mugs' Alley, beside the chairlift. Although it's over in about ten seconds it's well worth it just to ski deep powder through moguls, clinging to an almost vertical slope. At least if disaster strikes here you won't fall very far, and there are no rocks to worry about.

One of the great things about skiing Glencoe is that you can literally make up runs as you go along, and there's plenty of variety, from the very long east side runs to the headbangers' specials. On Mondays and Fridays you can practically have the hill to yourself and in any case, it's a very friendly place where everybody knows everybody else, so even queuing becomes enjoyable. At the end of the day, if conditions are good you can ski right down to the car park or even, if you've really got a lot of energy left, as far as the Kingshouse.

There is a snack bar at the foot of the Access Chairlift and another near the Cliffhanger Chairlift, where hot and cold drinks and snacks can be obtained. Also near the Cliffhanger you will find the Ski School and a shop. Further up, near the top of the Cliffhanger Chairlift, is the Scottish Ski Club Hut, which provides facilities for members only, and a short distance along on the same level is the Ski Patrol hut.

Nearest/latest petrol: Bridge of Orchy Garage, open 7.30am - 11pm Sunday to Thursday, and until midnight Friday and Saturday. In the other direction there is the Road to the Isles Fuel Station, Fort William, open 7am - 10pm weekdays, 7am - 1pm Saturday and 10am - 7.30pm Sunday.
Nearest breakdown services: Chisholms's Garage at Ballachulish, Tel. Ballachulish 557 (no fuel available) and MacRae & Dick at Fort William, Tel. 0397 2345

Enquiries about skiing at Glencoe from: White Corries Ltd., Main Office, The Ridges, Glencoe Ballachulish PH39 4HT Tel. 08552 303 (Ticket Office 08556 226)

GLENSHEE

The full extent of the Glenshee ski area is not immediately apparent on arrival. Having travelled through the splendours of Royal Deeside or negotiated the tortuous A93 from the south, the final climb to the car park brings one to a height of 2199 feet, which makes it the highest point in Britain to be reached by a main road. In the last few years the ski developments have extended not only over the slopes which are visible from the car park but into two further glens over the back of Sunnyside, opening up excellent new runs for all grades of skier.

Back in 1949, in the good old days of Scottish skiing, the very first tow to be installed at Glenshee was on Mount Blair. This 'Mark One' of a series of many was a rope tow, the kind which shredded gloves and fingers indiscriminately, and was greatly frowned upon by those who considered that using mechanical uplift was cheating. Nevertheless, in spite of its propensity for lengthening arms, it proved increasingly popular and was the start of an expansion from the fifties onwards, which today sees a total of two chairlifts and twenty-two draglifts, giving access to three glens and an enormous area of snow.

In spite of its size and popularity, Glenshee is a friendly resort. The runs are well-tended, and the wide-open spaces give a pleasantly uncluttered feeling, even when the tows are operating to capacity.

The first decision of the day is which side of the road to ski. Both sides offer a full spectrum of skiing for all abilities, but since the opening of the Glas Maol tow there has been an increasing tendency for the crowds to make a beeline for the Sunnyslope Chairlift in the mornings, leaving the Cairnwell side often without queues at all.

131

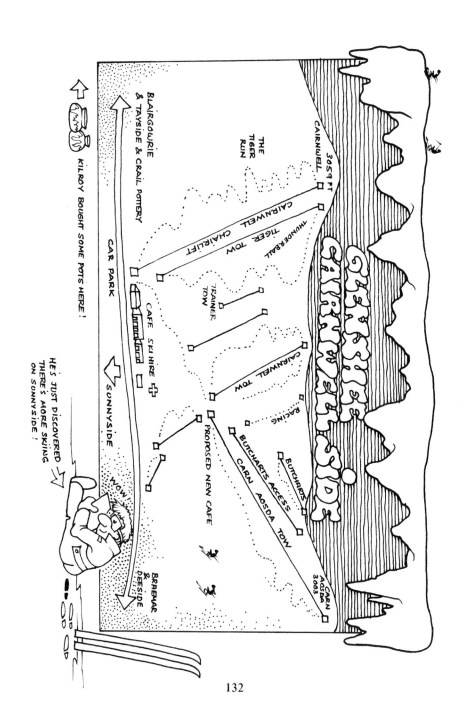

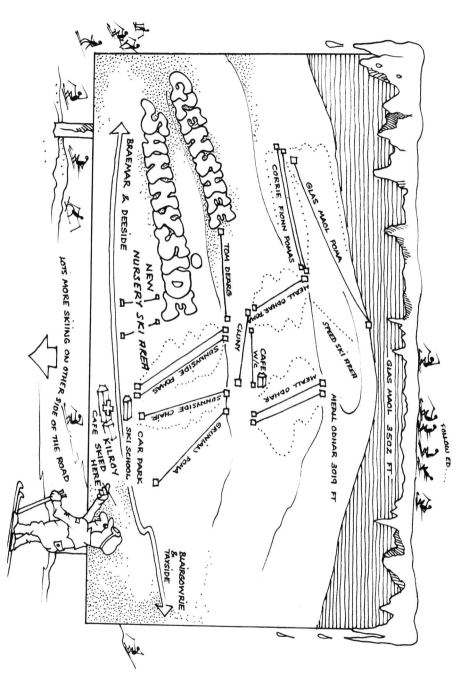

GLENSHEE SUNNYSIDE

GLAS MAOL POMA

CORRIE FIONN POMAS

MEALL ODHAR POMA

STEED SKI RFER

GLAS MAOL 3502 FT

MEALL ODHAR 3019 FT

MEALL ODHAR

CLUNY

CAFE W/C

TOM DEARG

SUNNYSIDE POMAS

SUNNYSIDE CHAIR

GRENIAS POMA

SKI SCHOOL

CAR PARK

KILROY CAFE SKIED HERE

NEW NURSERY SKI RFER

BRAEMAR & DEESIDE

LOTS MORE SKIING ON OTHER SIDE OF THE ROAD

BLAIRGOWRIE & TAYSIDE

FOLLOW ED.....

Starting with the slopes around the cafe, then, the choice of destination will depend largely on skiing experience.

For complete beginners, the nursery slopes adjoining the main car park or those of the Sugar Bowl, to the right of the cafe, are as good as any, provided you check that the run-out doesn't end in the burn, while for those who have found their feet and want to try a little uplift, the Trainer Tow on Cairnwell and the Ski School Poma are ideal. On the latter the ski school has priority, so at busy times it is well worth taking the Plastic Slope Tow or simply toning up the muscles in readiness for the day's punishment by walking up the hill to the Trainer Tow. Often the queues here are negligible, probably because of the walk, but the gradient is just right for the improving snowplougher.

At the top of the Plastic Slope Tow (which, incidentally, is no longer plastic) you will find the Carn Aosda T-Bar and the new Butcharts Access Poma in front of you, while the Cairnwell T-Bar is close by to the left.

For improvers, or for a pleasant warm-up, the Butcharts Access Poma is excellent, offering a number of possible descents depending on snow cover. Leaving the tow to the left, you can ski down beside it, pick yourself a route further out or follow the top snow fence along to the original Butcharts run.

Here there are two alternatives. For those who wish to avoid the short steep section at the top of Butcharts proper, it is possible to descend into a little bowl beside the upper tow and then cross the tow line. It is worth noting that often at this particular crossing point, riders of the T-Bar lose momentum and slide backwards for a few yards before the slack is taken up, hence there are a few close encounters with indecisive tow-crossers.

Although short, Butcharts usually holds its snow well, and the steep bit, reached by crossing above the top of the tow, is popular with budding short swingers. At the bottom you have the choice of going back up the T-Bar or returning down the flank of the gully to the Access Poma.

Carn Aosda, another T-Bar, offers a demanding run because of its steep and sometimes stony upper section.

The main run can be reached by turning left off the tow and side-stepping up to a broad, well-marked track which curves around the summit of the hill. Just before it meets the snowfence you break off to the left on a steepish traverse which will bring you to the fenced runs parallel to the tow. If the upper traverse doesn't take your fancy, you have the option of continuing on beside the snow fence to Butcharts.

More adventurous skiers can leave the Carn Aosda T-Bar to the right and ski a short way down a shallow gully before choosing whether to cross the tow and brave the often rock-studded steep bit or to head straight down and cross the tow on a lower section. It is also possible, when snow permits, for the expert to ski part-way round the shoulder and find a good descent. Sometimes early-morning powder can be found here: witness the graceful S-Trails left by the devotees of the 'steeps'.

The Cairnwell T-Bar provides access to the northern end of the Cairnwell ridge, giving a number of possible descents.

The first of these is the run to the left of the tow, steep and heavily mogulled at the top and running out to a longish level piste. Those who chicken out of the moguls and cruise along the ridge looking for a safer way down will find they have to contend with a cornice which, depending on snowfall, can have quite a considerable drop below it. In thick mist it is possible to miss the markers, so caution should be exercised here. If you go far enough along there are usually one or two tracks through it, pointing back towards the run, and these can be found by sideslipping carefully down.

On the right of the tow there is a blue (intermediate) run, quite narrow between the snowfences, where the race courses are laid out. Sometimes there is access to these, but when the course is set out you are asked to keep off. The public race course, which begins at a little A-framed hut, is operated by tokens which can be

135

Heed the Ice Warning

bought from the Cairnwell Ski School and can be used at any time there are not races in progress. The automatic timing device gives you a readout of your time when you reach the bottom.

Cairnwell is often used for racing, particularly at weekends, and at these times the racers have priority on the tow. This can make queueing frustratingly slow, so if you're liable to get upset about such things it's better to ski elsewhere.

A pleasant and easier route from the top of Cairnwell involves schussing down the side of the snowfence (don't be put off by the initial slope — there's a long run-out provided you can avoid the other skiers) and staying well up on the ridge until the next fenced run is reached. This often holds good snow and runs out slightly higher up the gully than the Butchart's Pass Poma. If you continue along the ridge you will find yourself traversing the slope facing Butcharts. Here the braver souls can peel off and practise their short swings down into the gully, where they may find a jump or two, whilst the scenic route continues to the head of the gully where it is possible to make an easy turn and cruise back down via the bottom of Butcharts.

The run for which Glenshee is most famous, the Tiger, is reached by either the Cairnwell Chairlift or the Tiger Tow.

Use of the chairlift, the single chair type, is for adults and older children only, and it should be remembered that in the space of a few minutes it can transport you from what seems to be a perfectly reasonable and pleasant day into near-Arctic conditions where it's almost impossible to stand upright for the ice-laden wind. Where you get onto the chair, in the tow operator's window, is a dial which gives the wind speed on the summit; it makes interesting reading. When the skull-and-crossbones 'ICE!' warning sign is out, it should be heeded, especially by anyone who will admit to being anything less than an expert skier.

There are times when the queue for the chairlift stretches right back up the gully, several rows deep, and it is quicker to shoulder your skis and walk up to the Tiger Tow, a fast-running T-Bar which takes you up to the Top Station. Whichever uplift you use, you have three choices at the top: to head off to the right along the ridge to Cairnwell, or to ski the right hand side of the Tiger Tow, or to ski the Tiger itself.

The traverse to Cairnwell can be reached by either of the tracks along the top of the ridge, and once on the traverse it is just a case of heading for where you think the route through the cornice might be. Groups of hesitant skiers dithering about taking the plunge over the edge will usually tell you.

When there is plenty of snow it is possible to pick out a number of routes back to the Tiger Tow by turning off before the traverse, but the black run descends close to the tow line itself. It's steep and narrow, with snowfences, pylons and rocks to avoid, so is definitely for better skiers only.

The Tiger itself is one of the best runs in Scotland. There are, of course, days when sheet ice, windslab and frozen, rutted moguls make it less than a doddle, but then maybe that's part of its attraction?

To get onto it you duck under the chairlift and immediately you're onto a broad and not-too-fierce slope where you can sort out the rhythm before the fun starts. After you've knocked the big moguls into shape you head for the narrower fenced run where the bumps are a more manageable size, and from there decide whether to head back to the T-Bar or the chairlift — or the cafe.

The eastern side of the road has developed beyond recognition since the early seventies. The always-popular Sunnyside tow is now a double poma, for which the queues continue to be long on busy weekends, and a double chairlift and a further poma, the Grunian, have been added. All the runs on the hillside adjacent to the road are blue (intermediate).

From the top of the Sunnyside Poma, there are three possible take-off points. Turning left off the tow, you can either ski the run nearest to it or take the slightly more level route northwards along the top of the hill and follow the next fenced run down. Both of these routes meet at the celebrated bottleneck where collisions, prone bodies and cries of 'Aaarrgggh!' are the order of the day. Those who survive it can confidently tackle the rest in the knowledge that the main hazards are behind them.

Turning right off the tow brings you to a slightly steeper run which joins part way down with one from the Sunnyslope Chairlift, and is a good route for those who wish to take the chair up next time. Though excellent when there is good snow, it is inclined to be patchy once the piste starts to wear thin, and picking the best route becomes an art. The wooden building at the foot of this run is the Scottish Ski Club Hut.

The Sunnyslope Chairlift is a double chair, on which children have to be accompanied by an adult. If you have a tribe of teenies, the lift attendant will normally slow the chair down for them to get on.

At the top, if you want to ski back towards the car park, you have three options. The first is to ski off to the left and after descending a couple of hundred metres take the right fork, which meets up with the run previously described. The left fork crosses under the chairlift and comes onto what is quite often a tricky descent initially, since it is not difficult to run out of snow. Lower down, as usual, things become more relaxed, and you can either rejoin the chairlift queue or cross over to the Grunian Poma. The descents from here are similar in nature to the last, and there is a turn-off to the left which takes you further along the car park if desired.

Over the back of Sunnyside are a number of green (easy) runs. From the top of Sunnyside Poma, you can ski straight over onto the Tom Dearg run, short and not too traumatic, but if you elect to go back up the Tom Dearg Poma remember to flex-ze-knees in readiness for a somewhat vigorous take-off.

Just below the top of the Tom Dearg run is a well-fenced traverse leading over to the Cluny tow, a double poma. Approaching from this point, you come onto the run halfway down, while direct access to the top of Cluny is from the chairlift.

Cluny is a great favourite with skiers at the snowplough stage, and holds few traumas, but for small children just beginning to get to grips with both skis and pomas, the gentle Beag tow is ideal. This runs from near the foot of Cluny and goes up to the Meall Odhar Cafe and toilets. A short ski/trudge from this point brings you to the Meall Odhar T-Bar and adjacent Caenlochan Poma.

Meall Odhar is one of the oldest runs at Glenshee, and for many years was the stronghold of the Dundee Ski Club, who developed the early tows there. The red runs to which the tows give access are excellent for fun and variety, often being mogulled at the top, and there are lots of different routes down which can be explored at will. Also, by taking the Caenlochan Poma rather than the T-bar, you can gain enough height to cross over to the Coire Fionn basin at the back.

The final tow on the Meall Odhar slope is the Meall Odhar Poma, just across from the bottom of Cluny.

Many skiers tend to use Meall Odhar Poma purely as a means of access to the Coire Fionn Basin, which can lead to a build-up in the queue at certain times. If you're heading over the back, then at peak periods it is often a good idea, when leaving the Sunnyslope Chair, to find a position from where you can scan the queue for the Caenlochan Poma, as it may provide a quicker alternative.

The full potential of the Meall Odhar Poma runs is, for some reason, largely untapped, which is a pity because some excellent red runs are available, especially on the north side of the tow.

To begin with the most obvious runs, however, you can leave the tow on either side. The right side has less consistent snow cover at the top, but when conditions are good it provides a steepish descent into mogulfields which tend to rapidly become cut into transverse ridges by skiers crossing the tow from the other side. Below here the run narrows and at the end of the day it is often scattered with spreadeagled bodies as the speed merchants catch up with the more cautious. It also has a character all its own at the end of the season when the underlying bog gobbles up skiers with relish.

Alternatively, by taking a high traverse round the shoulder of the hill, you can pick out one of a number of routes over to Caenlochan or the Meall Odhar Cafe. · To reach the former it is necessary to keep as high as you can initially, and since the traverse is fast and narrow, give the person in front plenty of time before you follow them.

Leaving the tow to the left, a short snow-fenced run leads to a wide-ish basin which becomes mogulled quite rapidly and provides good skiing when in condition. Most skiers descend near to the poma, crossing it at one of two possible points to reach the mogul slope mentioned earlier. The crossing places can become fairly congested by those rolling their eyes at the prospect of the hazards on the far side, particularly when the snow has drifted into a jump just next to the tow.

The north side of the tow has a lot of potential routes. By leaving the top basin to the right, or by taking the northern traverse from the Hairy Crossing, you will find a series of wide snowfields linked by narrow gaps in the rock and heather. It is worth exploring these: when the snow is good some superb descents can be had. If you intend to go back up Meall Odhar Poma keep an eye on your altitude and cut across at the appropriate level. If, perhaps at lunchtime or the end of the day, you are heading back to the car park, it is also possible to take a high traverse onto the slope facing the Cluny lift for a short, steep descent to the Tom Dearg Poma. 'Over the back', as the Coire Fionn/Glas Maol area has become known, there awaits a whole new spectrum of skiing.

Looking down from the top of the double Coire Fionn Poma, there are three main choices. The left hand route is the original run, and is deceptively smooth and easy at the top. Over the brow, however, things get interesting, with an excellent mogul run between the snowfences.

The other side of the pomas provides a descent of similar

gradient, but with more space to improvise, whilst the gentlest run of all is reached by a long traverse towards the head of the corrie. As you lose height you will notice a deep gorge below you, the well-known gun-barrel. Figures can be seen zig-zagging from side to side and occasionally popping out over the rim with a screech, a sport which soon becomes quite addictive. You need to keep your wits about you here, since it is preferable not to meet someone else 'to-ing' whilst you are 'fro-ing'. The more cautious can simply keep to the bank above.

The Glas Maol Poma provides some excellent runs for good intermediates upwards. The lift itself reaches right to the boundaries of a National Nature Reserve, hence the fluorescent markers beyond which skiers are banned. Ignoring the markers can lead to confiscation of your ticket.

At the top the only way off is to the left. Here there is ample space to adjust the lug-warmers and admire the view before taking any decisions about where to ski.

Immediately to the left is a gap in the snowfence. This leads onto the shoulder above the first black run and gives a fast descent which usually has good snow cover.

The wide schuss from the top of the tow leads to all the other routes. First left is the black run, marked 'Experts Only'. Narrow at first, it soon gives way to a wide, usually mogulled basin, with opportunities for some steep descents off the side walls. Further down you can choose between the gully and the slope above it, where sometimes powder lurks.

A second black descent is reached just beyond the mid-section of the ridgetop schuss, and is marked by a suitable gap in the snowfence. This is a steep descent of the shoulder, and is often at its best early in the day when you have the chance to make your own identifiable snake-trail. It provides some excellent skiing, but being less well-used, it can sometimes be subject to crusting, and may require crud-skills and stamina.

The main red run on Glas Maol is good for warming up on early in the day, and it tends to soften earlier because of its popularity. It begins with the afore-mentioned long schuss along the ridge between the snowfences, and since you want to get up a slight incline at the far end, if there is any sort of headwind you will need all the impetus you can muster at the start. Watch out, though, for skiers taking a sudden sharp left onto the black run.

The red run begins at the top of a wide horseshoe which can be descended from any point along the ridge. Good snow conditions make this an immensely popular playground, and it can absorb a surprisingly large number of skiers without seeming congested. In icy conditions the line down the gully is normally the first to soften up, although the unskied snow further along the ridge, while steep, usually provides a grip. At the foot of the gully is a minor gun-barrel which sometimes provides a take-off point for hot-doggers and also those engaged in less intentional aerobatics.

There are two cafes at Glenshee: one by the roadside at the foot of the Cairnwell and the other at the foot of Meall Odhar. Both serve sustaining fare and a good variety of beverages. (A hot sausage roll washed down with hot chocolate does wonders for the jeely-knees). To avoid queues at peak times there is a lot to be said for taking an early or late lunch, since not only do you avoid cafe pile-ups, you also get the benefit of diminished lift queues for an hour or so. Both cafes provide toilets and the car park complex also houses ski hire, a repair shop, the ski school, police and first aid posts and an equipment shop.

The nearest/latest petrol stations are: The Spittal Hotel, Spittal of Glenshee. Petrol (not diesel) available 24hrs. (provided the tanker has been!)
Grants of Braemar: normal opening hours for fuel plus 24hr breakdown service, Tel. 03383 301.
Latest fuel in Blairgowrie is from Lamb & Gardiner, open 7.30am - 9pm (8am on Sundays) and Norman Laing, Perth Street, also open until 9pm.
Breakdown service - Tel. Lamb & Gardiner, 0250 3501.

For enquiries about skiing at Glenshee contact:
Glenshee Chairlift Company Ltd., Cairnwell Mountain, By Braemar, Aberdeenshire AB3 5XU
Tel. 03383 320 (Office), 03383 628 (Snowline) - (033 9741 628 after Telecom change)

THE LECHT

The Lecht is a little over 50 miles from Aberdeen, which is the nearest major city. A small but very new Scottish ski area, it has steadily expanded and become increasingly attractive to skiers over the years. It is best suited to the beginner-to-intermediate skier and is especially good for families. It has also started its own Race Training School, which has proved to be a great success.

When you arrive at the car park, the first thing to strike you is that beginners do not have to walk any distance to the nursery slopes.

For the next stage, four tows are at hand — the Robin, Wren, Petrel and Kestrel. There will also be two new tows added to the system for the 1988/89 season, which tie in extremely well with the four mentioned above. All of these are green runs.

For blue runs, you have the Grouse, the longest at this standard, plus the Eagle, the most popular, and the Osprey. These runs are very varied, having gentle slopes, short steep sections and quite often small, well-formed moguls.

On the right hand side of the Eagle, a permanent race course can be seen and used by the general public. (Enquiries to the ticket office.)

Moving on to red runs, the Falcon and Buzzard lifts supply good skiing for the intermediate skier. The Falcon starts gently and increases in steepness as you descend. The moguls which form on this slope test the intermediate skier for flex and edge, and if worked hard enough, should considerably improve mogul technique. Ski School is strongly advised in order to eliminate bad habits.

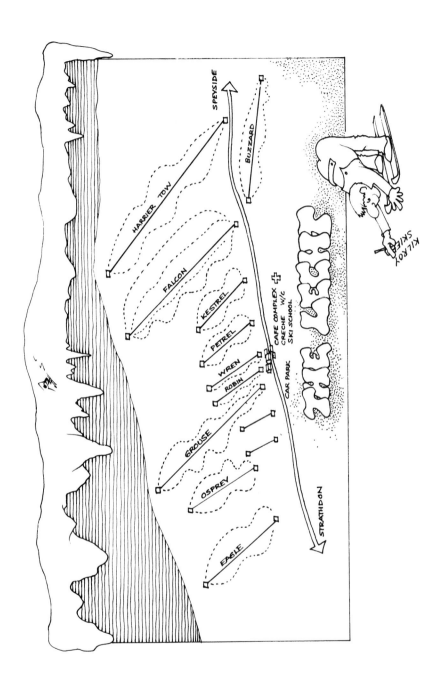

On the shorter side of the slope is the Buzzard, which is much steeper all the way down and often has some of the best snow. A must for the competent intermediate, it is also approved by the Scottish National Ski Council (SNSC) for races up to National Slalom level.

The last run on the system is the Harrier, the longest and steepest run in the range and is termed 'Proposed Racing Run' which speaks for itself.!

All the runs are well linked, and very little walking is necessary, and although this resort is best suited to families and intermediate skiers, the advanced skier should never forget that he is always learning: the Lecht is the ideal area for improving at all standards. Race training classes are open to all age groups, run by ex-British team coach John Clark, and there are also special courses for children aged twelve and under. There are ski races every weekend during the season, which anyone may enter.

The facilities in the area are very good and clean. Food is of a good standard and there is also room in the cafe at the rush-hour. Ski Hire, Ski School and a creche — yes, a creche — are all situated in the centre of the two car parks. The Lecht Ski Bus runs at weekends from Aberdeen: for details contact the Ski Swop Shop, 80 Huntly Street, Aberdeen (0224) 633533.

Nearest/latest fuel from: Grants of Tomintoul, open daily from 8am - 6pm and 11am - 6pm Sunday. They also run a 24hr breakdown service. Tel. Tomintoul 249.

In the other direction is Masseys Garage, Rough Park, Strathdon. Opening hours are 8am - 9pm Monday to Friday, 8am - 6pm Saturday and 10am - 6pm Sunday. Breakdown service available within these hours.

Enquiries about skiing The Lecht can be made to:
The Lecht Ski Company Ltd., Lecht Ski Centre, Corgarff, Aberdeenshire. Tel. 09754 240 (09756 51440 after Telecom change)

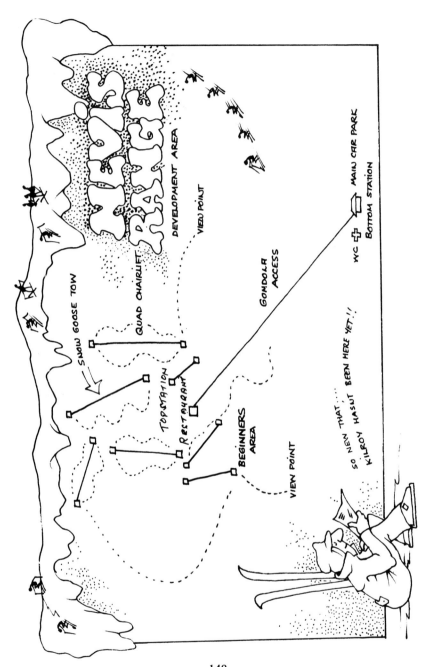

NEVIS RANGE

DEVELOPMENT AREA

VIEW POINT

SNOW GOOSE TOW

QUAD CHAIRLIFT

GONDOLA ACCESS

TOP STATION

RESTAURANT

BEGINNERS AREA

VIEW POINT

MAIN CAR PARK

WC

BOTTOM STATION

SO NEW THAT.....
KILROY HASN'T BEEN HERE YET.!!

148

NEVIS RANGE

The go-ahead was given in 1988 to the Nevis Range Development Company to develop Snow Goose Gully on Aonach Mor for skiing.

Set amid some of Scotland's most rugged and dramatic mountain scenery in an area which has a good snowfall record, the new development promises some exciting skiing for all standards, and will provide an excellent boost to the local economy.

Access to the ski area is to be by approximately ninety 6-seater gondolas, then by a four-seater chairlift and six tows. Two of these will be for beginners, set on a gentler slope a short distance away from the main skiing area. A high-capacity T-Bar will give access to the long, exhilarating pistes of Snow Goose Gully, from which the views are truly spectacular. Above this, a button tow will give access to the summit plateau.

Near the top gondola station will be the Snow Goose restaurant, seating 150, plus the ski school, ski workshop, childrens' area, garage, toilet blocks, shop and First Aid Room.

Reports on the progress of Nevis Range will be kept up to date by Ski Hotline, Tel. 0898 654 660.

Other enquiries to:
Nevis Range Development Company PLC,
Inverlochy Industrial Estate, Fort William,
Inverness-shire PH33 6LU.   Tel. 0397 5825

APPENDIX

MILEAGE CHART

	Cairngorm	Glenshee	Glencoe	The Lecht	Aonach Mor	Dalwhinnie Corries
Aberdeen	106	67	208	53	173	141
Dundee	106	42	96	77	116	72
Edinburgh	149	86	111	111	146	100
Glasgow	145	101	75	136	100	113
Inverness	47	97	130	62	95	64
Perth	89	41	74	76	99	56
Stirling	117	69	69	114	104	84

These distances are approximate, and are calculated using mainly Primary and 'A' Roads. They may not necessarily represent the shortest routes.

Petrol and breakdown information is given at the end of each specific ski area section, as are addresses of chairlift companies.

TOURIST INFORMATION CENTRES

Some smaller information centres may only be open on a seasonal basis or at weekends, but those in the larger population centres are open year round. If you telephone for information about acommodation and get an answering machine, it is worth leaving a message for details to be sent on.

AVIEMORE AND SPEY VALLEY TOURIST BOARD INFORMATION CENTRE, Main Road, Aviemore, Inverness-shire PH22 1PP. Tel. 0479 810363

BALLACHULISH TOURIST INTERPRETIVE CENTRE, Ballachulish. Tel. 08552 296

BLAIRGOWRIE TOURIST INFORMATION CENTRE, The Wellmeadow, Blairgowrie, Perthshire PH10 6AS. Tel. 0250 2960

BRAEMAR TOURIST INFORMATION CENTRE, Balnellan Road, Braemar. Tel. 03383 600

CARRBRIDGE INFORMATION CENTRE, Carr Road, Carrbridge, Inverness-shire. Tel. 0479 84 630

FORT WILLIAM TOURIST INFORMATION CENTRE, Cameron Centre, Cameron Square, Fort William. Tel. 0397 3781

GLENSHEE TOURIST INFORMATION, Corsehill, Upper Allan Street, Blairgowrie, Perthshire. Tel. 0250 5509

GRANTOWN-ON-SPEY TOURIST INFORMATION CENTRE, 54, High Street, Grantown-on-Spey. Tel. 0479 2773

INVERNESS TOURIST INFORMATION CENTRE, 23, Church Street, Inverness. Tel. 0463 234 353

KINCARDINE & DEESIDE TOURIST BOARD, 45, Station Road, Banchory, AB3 3XX. Tel. 03302 2066

KINGUSSIE TOURIST INFORMATION CENTRE, King Street, Kingussie. Tel. 05402 297

SPEAN BRIDGE TOURIST INFORMATION, The Caravan, Spean Bridge. Tel. 0397 81 576

TOMINTOUL MUSEUM, The Square, Tomintoul. Tel. 08074 285

BIBLIOGRAPHY/READING LIST

Ali Ross on Skiing   Ali Ross   (George Weidenfeld & Nicolson)
Avalanche Awareness for Skiers and Mountaineers   Epp and Lee
Avalanche Safety for Skiers and Climbers   Tony Daffern (Diadem)
Avalanche and Snow Safety   Colin Fraser   (John Murray)
Avalanche Symposium Report   (Alpine Club)
British Ski Federation Guide to Better Skiing   Samuel, Sheddon & Hynes
Cairngorms at the Crossroads   The Scottish Wild Land Group
The Cairngorms   Nethersole-Thompson & Watson (The Melven Press)
A Chance in A Million?, Scottish Avalanche   Barton/Wright
Competing in Cross Country Skiing   Nilsson (Oak Tree Press)
The Complete Ski Handbook,   Heller & Godlington (Martin Dunitz Ltd)
Cross-Country Skiing   Gillette/Dostal   (The Mountaineers, Seattle)
Cross-Country Skiing   Crawford-Currie   (Pelham Books)
Cross-Country Skiing   Field/Walker   (The Crowood Press)
Environmental Design and Management of Ski Areas in Scotland   CCS/HRC
First Aid for Hillwalkers and Climbers   Renouf & Hulse (Cicerone Press)
Free-Heel Skiing   Parker (Diadem Books)
Heading for the Scottish Hills   MCF/SLF (Scottish Mountaineering Trust)
Medicine for Mountaineers   Wilkenson (The Mountaineers, Seattle)

Mountain Craft & Leadership   E. Langmuir (Cicerone Press)
Mountain Navigation   Peter Cliff (D.E Thompson)
Mountain Navigation Techniques   Kevin Walker (Constable)
Mountain Skiing   Vic Bein (The Mountaineers, Seattle)
Mountain Weather   David Pedgley (Cicerone Press)
National Planning Guidelines 1984   Scottish Development Department
Nordic Skiing Manual - B.A.S.I. Manual
Safety on Mountains   British Mountaineering Club)
Scottish Mountaineering Club District Guide Books
Ski the Nordic Way   Cameron McNeish (Cicerone)
Ski Instruction & Technique - B.A.S.I. Manual
Ski Mountaineering in Scotland   Bennet & Walker (SMC)
Ski Tours Over Perthshire Hills   R. Simpson   (Ptarmigan Press)
Skiing - An Art, A Technique   Georges Joubert (Poudre)
Skiing - Developing Your Skill   John Sheddon (The Crowood Press)
Skiing Real Snow   Martyn Hurn (The Crowood Press)
Skiing School   Mark Heller   (Queen Anne Press)
Skilful Skiing   John Sheddon (EP Publishing Ltd)
Twenty One Years of World Cup Ski Racing   Serge Lang

USEFUL ADDRESSES

British Association of Parascending Clubs, 18 Talbot Lane, Leicester LE1 4LR 0533 530318

British Association of Ski Instructors, Grampian Road, Aviemore PH22 1RL

British Association of Ski Patrollers, C/o R.G.I.T. Survival Centre, 352 King St. Aberdeen. ★

British Red Cross, 9 Grosvenor Crescent, London SW1X 7EJ 01 235 5454 ★

British Ski Club for the Disabled, Corton House, Corton, Warminster, Wilts BA12 ONZ 0985 50321

British Ski Federation, Brocades House, Pyrford Road, West Byfleet, Surrey KT14 6RA 0932 3364 88

Countryside Commission for Scotland, (CCS), Battleby, Redgorton, Perth PH1 3EW 0738 27921

Data Ski Care (Ski Wax Specialists), 38, Rowan Drive, Westhill, Aberdeenshire. 0224 741859

Disabled Ski Club, Sec. Mr James Gebbie, 5 Drumsheugh Gardens, Edinburgh EH3 7QJ Tel. 031 225 5710 (Principally active in fields of physically disabled and blind skiers)

Highland Scottish Buses, (Ski Bus timetable), Railway Station, Aviemore 0479 810658

Hi-Line, Dingwall, Ross-shire IV15 9SL 0349 63434. Booking agency for Scottish skiing holidays — ask for Ski Holidays brochure.

Kandie Imports (Ski Maintenance Equipment), Candiehead, Avonbridge, Falkirk. 0324 86296

Nature Conservancy Council, 12 Hope Terrace, Edinburgh EH9 2AS

Outward Bound Trust, Chestnut Field, Regent Place, Rugby CV21 2PJ

Scottish Landowners Federation, 18 Abercromby PLace, Edinburgh EH3 6TY

Scottish Association of Snowboarding, c/o Marywell Gas, Stonehaven Road, Aberdeen.

Scottish Wild Land Group, 1/3 Kilgraston Court, Kilgraston Road, Edinburgh.

Scottish Wildlife Trust, 25 Johnston Terrace, Edinburgh EH1 2NH

Scottish National Ski Council, Caledonia House,South Gyle, Edinburgh EH12 9DQ   Tel. 031- 317 7280

Scottish Ski Club, Mrs J Lindsay-Bethune, 'Huircamdus', Elie, Leven, Fife KY9 LHD

Scottish Sports Council, 1 St Colme Street, Edinburgh EH3 6AA

Scottish Tourist Board, 23 Ravelston Terrace, Edinburgh.   Tel. 031 332 2433

Ski Club of Great Britain, 118, Eaton Square, London SW1W 9AF

St Andrew's Ambulance Association, 48 Milton Street, Glasgow G4 OHR.   Tel. 041 332 4031 ★

St John Ambulance, 1 Grosvenor Crescent, London SW1X 7EF   Tel. 01 235 5231 ★

Tayside Mountain Rescue, 12 Hazel Road, Dundee.

Uphill Ski Club, Ms Patricia MacLaurin, Overgare, Stuckenduff Road, Shandon, Dumbartonshire G84 8NW. Tel. 0436 82 0084 (Principally active in fields of cerebral palsy and mental handicap)

★ For details of first aid courses.

TABLES OF INJURIES ON SCOTTISH SKI SLOPES

Percentage distribution of types of accident

	Fall on piste	Fall due to terrain	Collision with skier	Collision with fence	Chairlift and towbar
Cairngorm					
Adults	70	7	7	10	6
Children	67	10	10	8	5
Glenshee					
Adults	65	15	8	8	4
Children	64	20	7	4	5
Overall	67	12	8	8	5

Distribution of injury for male and female adult skiers

Injury Subgroups	Specific Injuries	Female number (%)	Male number (%)
All upper body		172 (47.8)	323 (58.4)
Head and neck		45 (12.5)	42 (7.6)
Shoulder		30 (8.3)	78 (14.3)
	Shoulder dislocation	14 (3.9)	52 (9.4)
Wrist and hand		41 (11.4)	65 (11.8)
Thumb		22 (6.1)	51 (9.2)
	Ulnar collateral ligament	5 (1.4)	26 (4.7)
All lower limb		188	230
Knee		89 (24.7)	92 (16.6)
	Medial collateral ligament	44 (12.2)	42 (7.6)
Tibial fractures		30 (8.3)	57 (10.3)
Ankle		39 (10.8)	34 (6.1)
	Ankle fractures	20 (5.6)	17 (3.1)
Laceration/contusion		35 (9.8)	67 (12.1)
Other		29 (8.1)	66 (12.0)
TOTAL		360 (100)	553 (100)

Distribution of injury for male and female children skiers

Injury Subgroups	Specific Injuries	Female number(%)	Male number(%)
All upper body		62(34.4)	81(26.1)
Head and neck		16 (8.9)	12 (3.9)
Shoulder		10 (5.5)	21 (6.8)
	Fracture upper humerus	6 (3.3)	10 (3.2)
Wrist and hand		19(10.6)	16 (5.2)
Thumb		8 (4.4)	23 (7.4)
All lower limb	118	229	
Knee		30(16.7)	50(16.1)
	Medial collateral ligament	12 (6.7)	20 (6.5)
Tibia		49(27.2)	124 (40)
Ankle		20(11.1)	27 (8.7)
	Ankle fractures	11 (6.1)	13 (4.2)
Laceration/contusion		24(13.3)	26 (8.4)
Others		4 (2.2)	11 (3.5)
TOTAL	180	310	

LUATH PRESS GUIDES TO WESTERN SCOTLAND

SOUTH WEST SCOTLAND. Tom Atkinson.

A guidebook to the best of Kyle, Carrick, Galloway, Dumfries-shire, Kirkcudbrightshire and Wigtownshire.

This lovely land of hills, moors and beaches is bounded by the Atlantic and the Solway. Steeped in history and legend, still unspoiled, it is a land whose peace and grandeur are at least comparable to the Highlands.

Legends, history and loving descriptions by a local author make this an essential book for all who visit — or live in — the country of Robert Burns.

ISBN 0 946847 04 9. Paperback. £2.95p.

THE LONELY LANDS. Tom Atkinson.

A guide book to Inveraray, Kintyre, Glen Coe, Loch Awe, Loch Lomond, Cowal, the Kyles of Bute, and all of central Argyll.

All the glories of Argyll are described in this book. From Dumbarton to Campbeltown there is a great wealth of beauty. It is a quiet and lonely land, a land of history and legend, a land of unsurpassed glory.

Tom Atkinson describes it all, writing with deep insight of the land he loves. There could be no better guide to its beauties and history. Every visitor to this country of mountains and lochs and lonely beaches will find that enjoyment is enhanced by reading this book.

ISBN 0 946847 10 3. Paperback. Price: £2:95p.

ROADS TO THE ISLES. Tom Atkinson. A guidebook to Scotland's Far West, including Morar, Moidart, Morvern and Ardnamurchan.

This is the area lying to the west and north-west of Fort William. It is a land of still unspoiled loveliness, of mountain, loch and silver sands. It is a vast, quiet land of peace and grandeur. Legend, history and vivid description by an author who loves the area and knows it intimately make this book essential to all who visit this Highland wonderland.

ISBN 0 946487 01 4. Paperback. £2:50p.

THE EMPTY LANDS   Tom Atkinson.

A guidebook to the north-west of Scotland, from Fort William to Cape Wrath, and from Bettyhill to Lairg.
This is the fourth book in the series *Guides to Western Scotland*, and it covers that vast empty quarter leading up to Cape Wrath.   These are the Highlands of myth and legend, a land of unsurpassed beauty where sea and mountain mingle in majesty and grandeur.   As in his other books, the author is not content to describe the scenery (which is really beyond description), or advise you where to go.   He does all of that with his usual skill and enthusiasm, but he also places that superb landscape into its historical context, and tells how it and the people who live there have become what we see today.   With love and compassion, and some anger, he has written a book which should be read by everyone who visits or lives in — or even dreams about — that empty land.
ISBN 0 946487 13 8.   Price £2:95p.

ALSO FROM LUATH PRESS.

WALKS IN THE CAIRNGORMS.   Ernest Cross.

The Cairngorms are the highest uplands in Britain, and walking there introduces you to sub-arctic scenery found nowhere else.   This book provides a selection of walks in a splendid and magnificent countryside —there are rare birds, animals and plants, geological curiosities, quiet woodland walks, unusual excursions in the mountains.
Ernest Cross has written an excellent guidebook to these things. Not only does he have an intimate knowledge of what he describes, but he loves it all deeply, and this shows.
ISBN 0 946487 09 X   Paperback.   £2:50p

POEMS TO BE READ ALOUD: *A Victorian Drawing Room Entertainment.*   Selected and with an Introduction by Tom Atkinson.

A very personal selection of poems specially designed for all those who believe that the world is full of people who long to hear you declaim such as these.   The Entertainment ranges from an unusual and beautiful *Love Song* translated from the Sanskrit, to the drama of *The Shooting of Dan McGrew* and *The Green Eye of the Little Yellow God,* to the bathos of *Trees* and the outrageous bawdiness of *Eskimo Nell.*   Altogether, a most unusual and amusing selection.
ISBN 0 946487 00 6. Paperback.   Price £2:50p.

THE CROFTING YEARS. Francis Thompson.

A remarkable and moving study of crofting in the Highlands and Islands. It tells of the bloody conflicts a century ago when the crofters and their families faced all the forces of law and order and demanded a legal status and security of tenure, and of how gunboats cruised the Western Isles in Government's classic answer.

Life in the crofting townships is described with great insight and affection. Food, housing, healing and song are all dealt with. But the book is no nostalgic longing for the past. It looks to the future and argues that crofting must be carefully nurtured as a reservoir of potential strength for an uncertain future.

Francis Thompson lives and works in Stornoway. His life has been intimately bound up with the crofters, and he well knows of what he writes. ISBN 0 946487 06 5. Paperback. Price £4:75p.

TALL TALES FROM AN ISLAND. Peter Macnab.

These tales come from the island of Mull, but they could just as well come from anywhere in the Highlands or Islands.

Witches, ghosts, warlocks and fairies abound, as do stories of the people, their quiet humour and their abiding wit. A book to dip into, laugh over and enthuse about. Out of this great range of stories a general picture appears of an island people, stubborn and strong in adversity, but warm and co-operative and totally wedded to their island way of life. It is a clear picture of a microcosmic society perfectly adapted to an environment that, in spite of its great beauty, can be harsh and unforgiving.

Peter Macnab was born and grew up on Mull, and he knows and loves every inch of it. Not for him the 'superiority' of the incomer who makes joke cardboard figures of the island people and their ways. He presents a rounded account of Mull and its people. ISBN 0 946487. Paperback. Price: £5:95p.

HIGHLAND BALLS AND VILLAGE HALLS
G.W. Lockhart.

There is no doubt about Wallace Lockhart's love of Scottish country dancing, nor of his profound knowledge of it. Reminiscence, anecdotes, social comment and Scottish history, tartan and dress, prose and verse, the steps of the most important dances — they are are all brought together to remind, amuse and instruct the reader in all facets of Scottish country dancing. Wallace Lockhart practices what he preaches. He grew up in a house where the carpet was constantly being lifted for dancing, and the strains of country dance music have thrilled him in castle and village hall. He is the leader of the well-known *Quern Players*, and he composed the dance *Eilidh MacIain*, which was the winning jig in the competition held by the Edinburgh Branch of the Royal Scottish Country Dance Society to commemorate its sixtieth anniversary.

This is a book for all who dance or who remember their dancing days. It is a book for all Scots. ISBN 0 946487 12 X. Price: £3:75p.

BARE FEET AND TACKETY BOOTS. Archie

Cameron. The author is the last survivor of those who were born and reared on Rhum in the days before the First World War, when the island was the private playground of a rich absentee landowner. Archie recalls all the pleasures and pains of those days. He writes of the remarkable characters, not least his own father, who worked the estate and guided the Gentry in their search for stags and fish. The Gentry have left ample records of their time on the island, but little is known of those who lived and worked there. Archie fills this gap. He recalls the pains and pleasures of his boyhood. Factors and schoolmasters, midges and fish, deer and ducks and shepherds, the joys of poaching, the misery of MacBraynes steamers — they are all here.

This book is an important piece of social history, but, much more, it is an enthralling record of a way of life gone not so long ago, but already almost forgotten.

ISBN 0 946487 17 0. Price: £5:95p.

MOUNTAIN DAYS AND BOTHY NIGHTS. Dave

Brown and Ian Mitchell. The authors of this book have walked climbed and bothied over much of Scotland for many years. There could be no better guides to the astonishing variety of bothies, howffs and dosses on the Scottish hills. They were part of the great explosion of climbing in the Fifties and Sixties, and they write of it from first-hand knowledge.

Fishgut Mac, Desperate Dan, Stumpy and the Big Yin may not be on the hills any more but the bothies and howffs they used are still there. There was the Royal Bothy, paid for by the Queen herself after an encounter with a gang of anarchist republican hill-climbing desperadoes. There was the Secret Howff, built under the very nose of the disapproving laird and his gamekeepers. There was the Tarff Hotel, with its Three Star A.A. rating. These, and many more, feature in this book, together with tales of climbs and walks in the days of bendy boots and no artificial aids.

A delightfully nostalgic view of what the Scottish hills were like so short a time ago.

ISBN 0 946487 15 4. Price: £5:95p.

Highways And Byways In Mull And Iona. Peter **Macnab.** In this newly revised guidebook to Mull and Iona, Peter Macnab takes the visitor on a guided tour of the two islands. Born and grown up on Mull, he has an unparalleled knowledge of the island, and a great love for it. There could be no better guide than him to these two accessible islands of the Inner Hebrides, and no-one more able to show visitors the true Mull and Iona.
ISBN 0 946487 16 2. Price £2:50p.

TALES OF THE NORTH COAST. Alan Temperley and the pupils of Farr Secondary School. This is a memorial to the great tradition of Highland story-telling. Told simply and unadorned, these tales range widely — there are historical dramas, fairy tales, battles and shipwreck, ghosts, Highland rogues, all in stories which have been told for generations round the fire-side.

The tales have been collected from the people of the area, by their own children, who have illustrated them. In addition, Alan Temperly has added a series of contemporary writings about the Clearances in Sutherland, a central feature of local history, and a tragedy whose effects are still felt and discussed.

ISBN 0 946487 18 9. Price £5:95p

Any of these books can be obtained from your bookseller, or, in case of difficulty, please send price shown, plus 50p. for post and packing to:-

**LUATH PRESS Ltd.,
Barr, Ayrshire, KA 26 9TN. U.K.**